august/95

To Mé & Allyson,

with love & best
wishes in your new
endeavours!

— Jim

ONCE AGAIN, AT FORTY

By Jim Shannon

Published by

GENERAL STORE
PUBLISHING HOUSE

1 Main Street, Burnstown, Ontario, Canada K0J 1G0
Telephone 1-800-465-6072 Fax (613) 432-7184

ISBN 1-896182-19-4
Printed and bound in Canada

Layout and Design by Leanne Enright
Cover Design by Tammy L. Anderson

General Store Publishing House gratefully acknowledges the assistance of the Ontario Arts Council and Canada Council.

Canadian Cataloguing in Publication Data

Shannon, Jim, 1941-

Once again at forty

ISBN 1-896182-19-4

1. Shannon, Jim, 1941 2. Teachers--Canada--Biography. I. Title

LA2325.S47A3 1995   371.1'0092   C95-900300-2

First Printing May 1995

Dedication

For Elaine, Michèle, Denise and David

CONTENTS

If you're at the point where you're more than a little dissatisfied with your life, then this book is addressed to you. It's not too late to change. You've likely already savoured many of our society's 'successes' and found them somehow lacking. You wrestle often with a nagging notion that there must be more in life. You're ready for something new.

If you feel 'the clock is ticking' as you go through your daily paces, then *ONCE AGAIN, AT FORTY* could be just what you need to give yourself that 'jump start,' get you on another track, devoid of the sameness that is starting to drive you crazy.

Ten years ago—after at least two years of agonizing soul-searching and mostly vain attempts to inject some newness and vitality into my career—I left a secure teaching job that had gone stale after almost twenty years and have spent my time travelling, working at different jobs and going through the not-always-easy task of forging a new life. I got a job as a major-league baseball reporter, travelled in India, Eastern Europe and the Caribbean, worked as a freelance writer, lived and worked in Africa and was even, briefly, a public servant in Ottawa. I've never lost sight of my objective: to rejuvenate my life.

I believe everybody can experience the excitement inherent in taking that plunge from staleness and routine into the new and stimulating. The twentieth century values of more work, more stress and more money have not served us well. In the eighteenth century, a person was satisfied with making a modest amount of money and then retiring to more worthwhile pursuits. We are all capable of changing from a life of too little leisure time and too much stress to one of greater freedom, tranquility and, paradoxically, excitement and adventure.

We are all unique; the steps you take to shake things up in your life will be different than those I took. But if you're feeling dissatisfied and find yourself in a rut, then you have to make changes. The writer, Robert Heinlein, put it well: "To stay young requires increasing capability to unlearn old falsehoods." I think he meant that what is right for us at one stage of our lives is probably not right at another. Hence, we have to "unlearn" the old, and replace it with the new, the more appropriate. It may not be easy to change, but it's essential—and exciting.

I hope the adventures and travels I share with you in *ONCE AGAIN, AT FORTY* will entertain and, more importantly, inspire you to get on with the next phase of your life. The time to start is now.

Taking The Plunge

I thought I should be feeling more fear than excitement. Here I was, about to do the unthinkable: throw up a twenty-year teaching career, with no idea whatsoever of how I was going to earn a living.

But I was as excited as I felt when I took my first airplane trip, bought my first car, or had my first sexual experience.

I had reasons to hang on to a good job. Though divorced five years before, I had two daughters, to whom I was very attached and for whose upbringing I was partially responsible. And I didn't have much of a 'nest egg,' though I had managed to accumulate some savings.

Why had I decided on such drastic action? I had simply 'dried up' as an English teacher.

Entering my department head's office, I noted my palms were beginning to sweat. I was more nervous than I realized.

After the usual pleasantries, I said, "Doreen, I've made a big decision."

"What's that, Jim?" she answered disinterestedly, shuffling papers on her desk. She probably expected some drivel about a different method of evaluating students or a change of date of some planned workshop on teaching writing.

"I'm quitting teaching," I practically blurted.

"What?" She forgot about her papers. I'm sure she suspected some type of a joke. I mean nobody ever just quits a cushy community college teaching job— not after as many years as I'd been around. The salary was excellent and the holidays practically unbelievable; I was 'free' for about twenty weeks every year!

"Yes, I'm leaving," I continued, now feeling not quite as shaky. "I'm going to see what life is like in the real world," I smiled.

"Oh, I'm sure you'll do fine," she said, having now composed herself, adding sardonically, "in the real world."

She, no doubt, was now calculating the money her department would save by my leaving; she'd hire an inexperienced teacher to replace me at half my salary.

"You're sure about this?" she asked, as if to give me one final chance to come to my senses. After all, this was probably not the first time some teacher had come into her office near the end of the term, threatening resignation. Teachers tend to get depressed occasionally. Perhaps I was simply temporarily distraught.

"Yes, I've done my thinking about this," I answered. "I want to do something different before it's too late. From time to time we should all take a quantum leap—change our whole reality-matrix and land ourselves in new and exciting territory."

I knew the last bit would irritate her, but I remembered all the inane education jargon that had emanated from Doreen's mouth at meetings over the years.

I conjured up the image of a sea of grey-haired English teachers having a staff meeting a few years hence, a view of the future I found frightening. It was time to move on.

"Well, the college will miss you," she said, not convincingly. "I just don't quite understand why you're doing this."

"Teaching just doesn't excite me any more," I said. "My heart isn't in it. I feel almost revulsion at the thought of facing even one more class."

I had had great enthusiasm for teaching in the earlier years, but that feeling had long since dissipated. I had come to find the job distasteful. Surely I could find something to do that I could throw myself into, or that I would find at least palatable. Bob Dylan had said in one of his songs, "He not busy being born is busy dying."

I had been busy dying as a teacher for too long now; I knew I needed a change.

I declined Doreen's offer of coffee, left my letter of resignation on her desk, and walked out of her office, my heart still pounding.

Baseball Fantasy

George Plimpton had done it. He got to play quarterback for the Detroit Lions, if only for a few plays from scrimmage. But he had done it—lived out a fantasy. He, like me, had been in his early forties; he had added a dash of spice to his life.

I didn't fantasize about having a three-hundred-pound lineman barrelling down on me. I had even outgrown my childhood wish of replacing Mickey Mantle in centrefield at Yankee Stadium. But I did have a Plimpton-like dream.

I wanted to be a major-league baseball writer and cover my favourite team, the Montreal Expos, for a daily newspaper. The problem was I didn't have any experience—unless some editor would count a few drama reviews and travel stories I had written some ten years before for a small Western Ontario paper. Dozens of trips to Montreal from my home in Ottawa to cheer on my team wouldn't count as experience either. I had, indeed, 'paid my dues,' suffered through countless losing seasons, but my challenge was to transpose being a fan into landing a job as a sportswriter.

In the middle of the first winter after leaving my teaching career, I conceived of a potential opening one cold February day while skating with my daughters on the Rideau Canal. It was an outrageous longshot. I had taken The Plunge six months before in order to rejuvenate my life. Not much had happened since. I had to go for it, farfetched as my idea was.

Brashly evading his secretary, I walked into the office of the editor of the *Ottawa Journal*, at that time one of two dailies in the city. Ottawa was in Montreal territory; the Expos, having shown signs of coming of age the previous season, drew well from the region.

My tack was to suggest that the *Journal* should have a full-time writer covering the Expos—the rival *Citizen* newspaper had already taken that step the previous season—and that I was just the man for the job.

After the scowling, Lou Grant-style editor voiced his scepticism about my sportswriter credentials, he at least refrained from kicking me out of his office. He chomped on his cigar.

"Geez, it's not a bad idea," he allowed, "but what I really need is a 'name' writer, somebody with experience, not a bloody ex-English teacher. And how the hell do I know you can even write?"

"Read these," I said, passing him my slim portfolio containing nary a sports story in the lot. "And I know I can write baseball if you just give me a shot."

His parting words to me were, "Listen, I'm looking for experience, but you can show me what you can do in the meantime. Write me some baseball stories."

In February! Not an easy task, I thought, as I left his office. I felt only a hint of encouragement as I trudged home through the snow and slush, visualizing in my mind's eye sitting in the dugout at Olympic Stadium interviewing Gary Carter after batting practice.

Like the suitor encouraged by the slightest smile from the object of his affections, I hurried home that night to continue my wooing. I set out to write baseball stories, make-believe articles that would never be published. Maybe they would never even be read by the surly editor. The little I did know about journalistic writing told me that the odds were against my writing a good piece: there was no game to report on, no players to interview, no controversial items to report. I had only my imagination to rely on. Still, the image of Carter and me, side by side, wouldn't go away.

I likened myself to the rookie from the minor leagues trying to win a spot on the roster in spring training. And so that was what my first article was about. I mailed it off, having conjured up a picture of a young man from the Midwest boarding a bus bound for the Expos spring-training camp in West Palm Beach.

Next, I delved into my reservoir of "Expos facts and trivia," gathered over years of being a true fan. I knew there would be a battle that spring for the first-base job. A recently acquired, aging star would be trying to unseat a seasoned-if-unspectacular veteran. I made up an article about that and mailed it off.

It was not difficult for me to imagine the feud that would likely develop between testy manager, Dick Williams, and his ace pitcher, Steve Rogers, who would be coming back after elbow surgery and would be acting even more prima donna-like than usual. Or the heroic attempt by a sore-armed lefthander trying to make a comeback. It was almost like the creative writing assignments I used to give my students.

Unlike my students, however, I got no marks for my work. A month went by and I had heard nothing from Mr. Editor. Perhaps he'd had a good laugh about me and my baseball writer aspirations. Maybe he had already hired his experienced writer. Perhaps he had tossed my stories into his wastebasket. Still, I kept churning them out.

In late March, I got a call. It wasn't exactly like being summoned from the bullpen after warming up game after game, but I felt a glimmer of hope. He wanted to talk to me.

"Well, you show some promise," he said, cigar clenched between teeth. "I can tell you know the game well, and I think your stories would have more impact if you had access to the field, the locker room and so on. You have a hell of an imagination, I have to say."

He told me he was still hunting for an experienced sportswriter, but that I should keep those stories coming. He'd get back to me soon.

I felt that I had at least made the forty-man spring training roster, if not the team. I was in the running. I felt hopeful, almost elated. My foot was in the door.

Spring training was in full swing in Florida, and I pored over newspapers, looking for story ideas. I'd use a scant one-liner in a report and concoct an article from it. For example, when eccentric pitcher Bill Lee announced that he disliked playing on artificial turf, I made up an article about the inevitable clash between Lee and Expos' management: "Pitcher Refuses to Play on Carpet," a stand that stirred up the Expos' brass no end as half the parks in the league would be off-limits to the flaky pitcher!

To my amazement, only a few days before the Home Opener, I got a call from the *Journal.*

A week later, I found myself riding the elevator to the press box at Olympic Stadium in Montreal, baseball-writing credentials in hand. I had been given a one-month tryout! Sixteen home games to cover. No more make-believe stories. This was the real thing. My knees were wobbly.

Joining the other writers, I was acutely aware of being a greenhorn. I didn't even know what a sportswriter was supposed to wear—a tie, a jacket? I had not been told how to file my story. Did writers use telephones or some sort of electronic device? I had refrained from asking questions so as not to reveal my ignorance. And deadlines—how was I going to handle them? How would I manage to file my game story within a half-hour or so of the end of the game when even my typing skills were poor?

Having to show up in class on time was hardly a gut-wrenching deadline. This was all new to me. I felt some anxiety.

I didn't feel out of place for long though. Expos play-by-play announcer Dave Van Horne greeted me with a cheerful "Hi," and his partner, Hall-of-Famer Duke Snider, nodded pleasantly. Duke Snider! I could hardy believe I was standing next to this baseball legend, a man I had idolized when he played for the old Brooklyn Dodgers back when, as a twelve-year-old, I used to fool my mother into thinking I was asleep while listening to the exploits of the Duke and Jackie Robinson and Gil Hodges on a radio under my pillow. And here I was—eating a hot dog, shoulder-to-shoulder with the Duke himself.

The San Francisco Giants were the Expos' opponents that day. I took my seat at the end of a row of writers in the press box. I felt like the kid just called up from the minors—very nervous. But as soon as the game started, the butterflies went away, just the way a rookie's do.

I kept score, made notes of highlight plays for my story. It was all a bit overwhelming. Especially when I made a beeline with the other writers to the locker room after the game, to get some hurried quotes from the game stars and the managers.

I was awestruck. My pad in hand, I couldn't get anything down as I glanced around the room, spotting André Dawson eating a piece of chicken, Gary Carter quietly sipping a beer, answering reporters' questions patiently. Ellis Valentine, long one of my favourites, whizzed a wet towel by my head as he exited the showers. Pitcher Steve Rogers held court, his arm encased in a bag of ice, another win chalked up.

"Yes, I made a mistake when I got the fastball up and in to Jack Clark," he explained, sounding more like a doctor accounting for a surgical blunder than a grown man playing a kids' game. No matter, the Expos had won even if Clark had deposited the pitch high into the bleachers for a three-run homer.

As I scribbled feverishly now, feeling the pressure of having to compose a story for tomorrow's paper, I was struck by the fact I was instantly accepted by writers and players alike. I was just a guy who had a job to do. Rogers threw pitches; I took notes. Yesterday I was a college teacher; today, a baseball writer. There was a sense of unreality about it all.

I managed to file my first story. I frantically made the paper's deadline. Here I was, poor typing skills and all, with only my driving passion to do the job. I finally understood what athletes meant when they spoke of feeling the adrenalin flow. I felt drained as I walked to my car in the stadium lot.

Still, I didn't know if the story would even be printed. But I had done it. I had gotten at least one game in the big leagues. I thought of George Plimpton taking the snap from his centre and seeing the three-hundred-pound lineman coming at him, but still managing to get rid of the ball, flinging it to a prospective receiver down field. It felt good.

The next morning, I headed for a news-stand. My hands shook as I groped for the sports section. My story was there! Right on the front page, by-line and all. I read the piece hurriedly. They hadn't changed a word. I was ecstatic.

I strolled down St. Catherine Street, paper tucked under my arm, and wondered what it would be like covering the World Series in October.

I never made it to the World Series that fall. Not only did the Expos drop out of the pennant race in late summer, my paper followed suit; it actually went out of business. In dramatic fashion, it announced in a front-page story on August 27, 1980, that it was folding with that very edition, citing economic reasons for its demise. I was not alone in my shock. Many career journalists were suddenly out looking for new jobs. I joined them, my venture into baseball writing curtailed after a short three months.

Even though I had proved I could do the job—I had been hired on as a full-fledged reporter after less than a month on the baseball beat—I did not have impressive credentials when thrown out on the open market. I was once again a forty-year-old with twenty years of teaching experience plus three months of sportswriting. Not only that, I didn't have the same enthusiasm now as I did a few months previously. Possibly the novelty had worn off.

A curious thing had been happening to me just as the newspaper folded. I had become less of a baseball fan and more of a reporter during my brief stint covering the Expos. I still liked the idea of being paid for something I loved to do, but I missed being a fan. I couldn't stand up and cheer in the press box. Indeed, as I got to know the players, I didn't see them as heroes any more. An outfielder who made a spectacular running catch took on an added dimension for me; he was also the arrogant, gold-chain-laden, cadillac-driving bore I tried to talk to after the game in an attempt to get him to say something quotable for my readers' enjoyment over breakfast the next day.

Not that I discovered all ballplayers to be self-centred illiterates; many were modest, co-operative and business-like. But few had much to say. It hit me suddenly one day, as I sat beside a star shortstop trying to get material for a feature story on him for a Saturday edition: these guys never say anything new. And then, I realized that there was no reason they should. They were skilled athletes. This shortstop, for instance, could make the double play like nobody on this planet. And there was no reason why he should be expected to talk about it articulately.

I watched veteran writers snooze during games, groan about how spoiled ballplayers were and arbitrarily divide up quotes which somebody scribbled down in order to dress up their stories. I was reminded of the cynical teachers I used to try and avoid in my former profession, the ones who should have quit years before.

I yearned to sit in the bleachers with my kids, or my friend Tom, and be a fan again.

Should a person make work out of a hobby? I was wrestling with that one when I awoke on that August morning to see the fateful headline:
"Last Edition —Journal Folding."

And so, I decided not to look for another sportswriting job. The memory of that first day at Olympic stadium was fresh; I wanted the adrenalin to flow again! Baseball isn't the only thing in life I can become excited about. Travel has always intrigued me too. In my soul-searching about what to do with my life, I decided to gravitate towards what stimulated and excited me.

I had gone through the sending-out-twenty-résumés routine, and realized that I wasn't finding anything to do because I didn't know what I was looking for. Having decided to be a teacher at age twenty, I had simply not plugged in to the real me over a period of twenty years of career, marriage, childrearing, etc. And my present state of being 'stuck' was fairly predictable. I was scared. I had no salary anymore, only a little savings. I wanted to contribute to the upbringing of my daughters whom I loved dearly. Still, I had made a commitment when I walked into Doreen's office. I was going to change my life.

So would it be travel? One voice in my head said, "Get established again, get back on the track." Another said, "Follow your instincts, don't stop now!" Travel won out.

Elaine, a woman I had been with for about a year, shared my enthusiasm to set off exploring the world. We agreed on a destination that was new to both of us, not overly travelled, culturally interesting and inexpensive—India.

Home of almost a fifth of humanity, India had loomed large in both our imaginations for years.

I planned to write some articles about our travels. But that objective was secondary. We wanted to finally see India—and not from a tour bus window.

For both of us, having recently taken the first step in changing our lives and yearning for something different and challenging, India seemed just what the doctor ordered!

India—More than Great Curries

And so, a week after deciding on India, Elaine and I found ourselves, arms still sore from a plethora of innoculations, boarding an Air India jet in Montreal, bound for New Delhi. We had sublet our apartment, said goodbye to family and friends, and reduced our necessities of life to what we could each cram into one shoulder bag.

Travelling light, we wanted the freedom to ride local buses and do a lot of walking. Aside from money, a passport, a toothbrush, a change of clothes and comfortable shoes, what does one really need when on the road?

The flight itself was a preview of India. Most of the passengers were Indian and the airline attendants were dressed in native garb. We ate pungent curries to the accompaniment of recorded sitar music. The stage was being set.

We were intimidated by India, nevertheless. Its sheer size was a daunting thought—eight hundred million people. How were we going to cope? As we walked out of New Delhi's airport at two in the morning, after twenty-two hours of flying time, I felt my stomach churning. We hadn't even made hotel reservations.

Throngs of people milled about outside the terminal even at that late hour. My sense of smell, dormant for months in the Canadian winter, came quickly to life. Food, vegetation and smoke mingled to help create the most exotic experience of our travel lives, and we had just stepped off the airplane!

What struck us most, as we looked for a bus into the city, was the dress of the people: the men in dhotis, the suit-like, loose-fitting garment so ubiquitous in India; the women bedecked in saris, the often-colourful, graceful attire made of only one piece of material, a bit over a metre in width and about six metres in length, draped over the shoulder and fastened with no pins or buttons. Throughout our travels, we were to marvel at the personal cleanliness and decorum of the people, in spite of the enormous problems of poor sanitation due to sheer numbers alone.

We refused dozens of offers of taxis, trying to convince drivers that we really did intend to use public transportation. And we got our desired bus, in due time —a half hour or so. Lesson number one: long waits, for everything, would be the rule in India.

Downtown New Delhi was eerily quiet. We had a map of the core area and a few ideas for budget hotels but, at three in the morning, we found most of these locked up with nary a soul in sight. We were tired and decided to let a taxi—a motorized three-wheeled rickshaw—take us to a hotel described by the driver as, "just up the hill, and very good with cheap price."

We climbed into the 'cab'—the two-seater behind the driver—and sped off at breakneck speed up the hill. The hill turned into a winding, almost moun-tain-like road, which our driver negotiated expertly as he held a cigarette in one hand and talked to us constantly, half-turned around.

Up one side of the hill and now careening down the other side, like a shot out of a cannon, twisting and turning, our taxi sped along. "Tomorrow I pick you up at hotel," the driver said, adding proudly, "I show you all of Delhi!"

We were now getting edgy. Would we end up in an Indian hospital our first night here? Elaine and I glanced at each other, probably both thinking of how we refused our Canadian travel agent's offer to book us a 'regular' hotel.

Eventually we arrived at our destination. All was in darkness. The driver pounded on the door. The building looked like an ordinary home. We were perplexed.

A door opened and a whispered conversation took place between a sleepy-eyed man and our taxi driver.

"Come," said the driver, after a time.

We followed dutifully, our fatigue having finally taken its toll. The proprietor said nothing. The driver said to me, "Forty rupees, good price," smiling, pleased with himself.

I was not about to argue about a sum equivalent to five Canadian dollars. Not even when we noticed, by the light of the moon beaming through the window, that there was no bedding provided. We carried our own sheet sleeping bags. The bed looked inviting and we fell asleep almost immediately.

I awoke to the aroma of cooking food. The smells were, predictably, foreign to my senses. Was it breakfast being prepared? Or had we miscalculated the time, waking up just in time for dinner?

There was a knock on the door. I opened it and was greeted by the outstretched hand of the man I had taken to be the proprietor when we arrived last night. Except now, instead of sleepy grumpiness, the man exuded warmth and charm.

"Welcome to my home, sir," he said. "You do me and my family a great honour in staying with us."

I thanked him for his welcome, apologized for waking him last night and accepted his invitation to have "a simple morning meal."

Our host, Colonel Bhanerjee, introduced his family—his wife, resplendent in her sari, and four daughters, all seemingly in their teens and very shy. I looked around for other guests; there were none. The house was spacious, but modest.

An array of food was placed before us by a server. Elaine and I, always eager to try new cuisines, eagerly plunged into the task at hand. It was a sumptuous breakfast. We simply followed the lead of our host, eating with our right hand, aided sometimes by a piece of chapati to spoon up any soup-like items, such as dhal or yogurt. The curries were magnificent; the fruit which followed, exotic. We stuffed ourselves—to the delight of our host.

"I expected you to protest," he said. "So many foreigners find Indian food excessively spiced."

"Your hospitality is wonderful," Elaine said. "We never expected anything like this."

"Well," said the Colonel, "since I retired from the service, I have grown to enjoy entertaining travellers. As you see, we take very few guests. Indeed, we have only the one room that is vacant."

I wondered what a military colonel was doing taking in guests. Surely it wasn't the money. Yet I doubted the reason was as simple as his enjoying our company.

We went into the garden to drink our coffee with our host.

The Colonel's wife and daughters had excused themselves to get on with their daily tasks. We realized that our rickshaw driver had given us an opportunity of a lifetime—to get inside an Indian home. Only later did the irony of this happening—within an hour of arriving in the country—strike us. Travellers might spend a year in the country and never get to meet socially with local people.

We listened with fascination to the Colonel's story. "I am a poor man," he said, sadly. "I have no hope, no way of escaping poverty in my old age."

"But you are a high-ranking officer," I protested, "and your house is attractive and comfortable."

"Yes, I see what you are thinking," Colonel Bhanerjee said. "And I have a pension, too. And, yes, I was even educated in England. I come from a caste called the Kshatriyas, just beneath the Brahmins."

I confessed my relative ignorance of the complicated Hindu caste system, recalling only that Mahatma Ghandi had put great effort into bringing the lowest caste, the Untouchables, into society, renaming them the Harijans, or Children of God.

"Indians are enslaved by this antiquated system," the Colonel went on. "It is more rigid the higher you go up the caste ladder. Its origins are lost in the mists of history, but, basically, it seems to have been developed by the Brahmins, or priest class, in order to make their own superior position more permanent. Eventually, the caste system became formalized into four distinct classes, each with rules of conduct and behaviour. In fact, though, there are dozens of sub-divisions within each caste."

He sighed, repeating, "I am a man without hope," adding, "at least in this incarnation."

"But why?" Elaine asked.

"My dear lady," he said, "you, no doubt, noticed my four daughters."

Yes, they're beautiful girls," she answered.

"Beautiful, yes. And I love them very much. But they spell disaster for me."

It dawned on me that I had read a story in a newspaper before leaving Canada which had caught my attention. It dealt with a dowry murder in a small Indian village. It seemed the groom and his family, upon discovering that the bride's family had falsely represented their wealth (revealing after the wedding that they did not, in fact, possess the six cows they had claimed to own), had arranged the murder of the bride, divorce being out of the question for devout Hindus.

"Is it really that rigid?" I said.

"Indeed, it is," the Colonel said. "If only I had a son or, better, two or three. I could provide a proper dowry for one, or even two of my daughters, but for four, it is impossible. And with no son to look after me in my old age, I am destitute."

"But," I asked, "since you seem not to even believe in the caste system any more, can't you just, well, introduce your daughters to sons of similarly less traditional parents?"

"It is impossible in Hindu society to bend the rules. Only complete ostracization would follow. You see, I am supposed to think my present incarnation is unimportant, that if I behave myself, accept my plight, then I may be better off in the next life I have here. Really, my friends, the caste system, and the caste system alone, is the heaviest burden India has to carry. It will be our doom."

"Couldn't you have your daughters bypass marriage, perhaps learn a profession, become self-sufficient?" I asked.

"Oh, sir, if only it were that simple. You see tradition is everything here. I have lived and studied in the West, but my wife and all our relatives have not. You and I see myself as somewhat enlightened, but they would see me as possessed of the devil. Hindus are first and foremost spiritual people. They would scoff at my concerns, scolding me for being materialistic and greedy and, worse, for attempting to step outside of my caste."

Elaine and I were silent.

"Forgive me for unburdening myself with you, my guests," he said. "It is unforgivable, but I feel so helpless. My wife and I never speak of such things. However, I thought you should understand the essence of Indian social customs."

"We're grateful for your candour," I said.

"Well, I think perhaps it may help you to understand the people as you travel around this country," the Colonel said and added wryly, "Perhaps I can travel to Canada sometime, but it will have to be in a different incarnation. I am doomed to be a poor man in this one."

Later, as promised, our rickshaw man picked us up, gave us a tour of the city and dropped us at the Delhi train station.

Varanasi — The Holy City Where the Band Played On

If a traveller were to have only one day in India and wanted to experience the essence of the country, he or she should visit Varanasi, the Holy City.

Elaine and I arrived in Varanasi late one night, after an all-day bus ride from Nepal. We had unavoidably created a problem for ourselves earlier in the day by running out of rupees. All along the bus route, we kept hoping that we'd spot a bank during one of the interminable stops. As villages and towns came and went, we found no such bank at which to change money. We had survived the day on the kindnesses of fellow passengers, all Indians, who offered us food and drink. With darkness, and the large city, ahead of us, we were feeling more than a little anxious.

Varanasi is the most important pilgrimage site in the country. Situated on the banks of the sacred Ganges, it has for two thousand years been a centre of learning and civilization. Hindus from across the land come here, not only to bathe in the Ganges, but to die here and, if they have the required funds, to be cremated on the river's banks, at one of the burning ghats.

Right now, we were not interested in watching pilgrims bathe in the holy river —or in gawking at the dead being burned along the river bank. We needed money. Credit cards were of no use in India.

At five o'clock, the streets were teeming with people, but the banks were now closed. A passenger had told us of the location of a large, Western-style hotel, often a place to cash travellers cheques in India. At the bus station, we settled on one of dozens of rickshaw drivers who vied for our fare—here they used bicycles to propel the 'taxis' along—and explained our dilemma to him. He probably thought we were joking when told we had no money and gladly set off for the Varanasi Ashok, the ritziest hotel in town. If things worked out, we'd then have our friendly driver drop us at an inexpensive tourist bungalow and we'd head straight for the nearest restaurant. We were starved.

We had learned to count on nothing in India, however, and when the officious clerk at the posh hotel informed us that the vault was closed for the night—"Impossible to open it"—we were not surprised. But no problem, we were told. We could stay there that night and wait until morning to pay. The rate? Oh, about ten times what we wanted to pay for a room.

We declined the clerk's offer. Urging on our rickshaw driver, we set out again through the streets of Varanasi. Surely, one of the other large hotels could help us. On the way, we saw amazing sights: funeral pyres burning along the Ganges; passing rickshaws with dead bodies accompanied by a family member; Hindu temples filled with pilgrims. And the smells—evening meals being cooked in the streets, mingled with the ever-present smoke from the burning ghats. It all made us forget our plight, and our hunger, for the moment.

After three attempts, we hit pay dirt. We got our rupees. Then we found a little hotel and rewarded our driver for his efforts. The process had taken two hours, but our frustrations at least included fringe benefits—we had enjoyed a first-class tour of the Holy City. Such was invariably our experience in India. Just when things got bad, they always got interesting.

We awoke at dawn and made our way to the Ganges. Sunrise, we had heard, was the best time to see Varanasi. The sights we were to glimpse that day would indelibly etch India in our minds.

Pilgrims, many of whom would have spent their lives dreaming of bathing in the sacred river, were there now by the hundreds. The women bathed discreetly in their saris. The men went through their yoga exercises, contortion-like. Brahmin priests went about offering blessings—for a price—and the ever-present beggars stood around giving others an opportunity to do their karma some good by giving a donation to the poor.

We saw a body being cremated at one of the ghats, or altars, near the bank. Just downstream, more pilgrims were bathing. Near every ghat were temples, some of which looked ready to tumble into the Ganges, tilting precariously after a heavy monsoon season had damaged the river bank. What was most striking were the expressions on the faces of the pilgrims. Ecstasy might be too strong a word, but serenity certainly fits.

Just then, a corpse arrived on the top of a taxi, the bereaved family following behind. Sounds of chanting emanated from nearby temples, smells of cooking drifted across the river. The city was coming to life. The contrasts were mind-boggling. This was India. The sixteen-hour bus ride was worth the effort.

That evening, after spending the day touring the city on foot, we met a couple from Toronto who told us that the famed Ravi Shankar, one of Varanasi's most renowned citizens, and a celebrity since he had led the Beatles to India—and the Maharishi—in the 1960s, was headlining a concert that very evening. Certainly, we were up for it, we told our new friends.

We were excited about attending a performance by the sitar player once described by John Lennon as the greatest musician in the world.

Promptly at eight that evening, we arrived at the auditorium, a rather sad looking place for an artist of such stature to be playing. It was barn-like, and had a hole in the roof through which the audience could see the stars. Since this was the dry season, we wouldn't be getting wet tonight.

We noticed that our section was quickly filled—with other tourists. It was odd being suddenly with more Westerners than we had seen in months. What was even odder was the fact that there were as yet no Indians present. Nor was there any sign of a concert about to begin.

An hour passed. All of us tourists looked at each other, nobody wanting to express any concern. Nobody joked, "Are our tickets for the next night, perhaps?" People were becoming restless and uncomfortable, sitting on the hard, straight-backed chairs.

Just before ten, after two hours, some Indians began to arrive. We noted their very fashionable dress. Upon finding their seats, they immediately headed for the bar, the presence of which was a rarity in Hindu India. Were we seeing the Indian answer to the liberated rock set?

By ten there was still no music. But a half-hour later, some musicians took the stage and started to warm up. Imagine six or seven sitar players all strumming at once; it was bedlam. And where was the star? Mr. Shankar was nowhere to be seen.

Gradually, the musicians began to jell. Sitars, in perfect harmony, filled the hall with the sound of India. But, even at eleven o'clock, there was still no Ravi Shankar. Pampered Western rock stars sometimes arrived late for the show, but this was ridiculous. The opening act begins two hours late and the star still fails to appear two hours later!

At about twelve-thirty, the crowd began to stir; something was obviously going to happen. Even the intensity of the music picked up.

Surprise! Another half-hour passed. Talk about foreplay! The audience was more than ready for Shankar. But was he ready for us? Apparently not—yet.

My body was aching after five hours of sitting. We had decided to leave at one o'clock if the star hadn't appeared by then. We'd chalk this one up to experience. At least the crowd was entertaining—a show in themselves—as they climbed over each other for beer or tea or pepsi.

Ravi Shankar did perform that evening, so we learned the next day from our Toronto friends who had stuck it out. The Great One appeared at two o'clock, amid much crowd hysteria, played for a half-hour, bowed to the audience and disappeared. There can be no doubt about it, Ravi Shankar is a big star in Varanasi. It seems his fellow citizens deemed his appearance, albeit a short one, a great honour.

Next time, we'd attend a concert Indian-style. We'd dine leisurely, and perhaps take in a movie first!

From the burning ghats along the sacred Ganges and the great river's almost palpable spirituality to the concert in which the band played on—with or without the star performer—we'd managed to savour the essence of India in one memorable day in Varanasi.

Oh, Calcutta!

Calcutta would probably not top the list of Recommended Oases For Tired Travellers. It conjures up images of starving street kids, lepers, beggars—in short, everything needed to make travel-weary people head for the nearest airline office. "Two tickets for Canada, please!"

We were catching on, however. Slowly, and somewhat painfully, we discarded our Western concepts of expectations and of time. Tackling India's largest city was nevertheless daunting. Calcutta had the most of everything in the country—people, poverty, slums, crime, disease. But it was reputed also to be the most fascinating of cities, with restaurants, museums, theatres galore—a treasure chest of Indian culture and history.

As the train came to a stop, Elaine and I stepped down onto the platform to be accosted by several porters pleading to carry our bags. We explained that "all our baggage" was what they were looking at—our tattered shoulder bags. They assumed we were being evasive and became mildly hostile. We did what we had both learned in many weeks of travel; we put our heads down and bulled our way to the street.

We wandered into the mass of people, looking for what we needed most—food. We were not disappointed and spotted a little restaurant immediately.

The food, as usual, was wonderful. Our spirits had been lifted once again. As we were getting ready to leave, a man nearby—he looked like a Sikh, turbanned, bearded and tall—came to our table.

"Hello, my name is Namur," he said, offering his hand. "Did you just arrive in Calcutta?"

I tried not to be abrupt, but I had heard his opener dozens of times in the past six weeks and I assumed he had something to sell at "very cheap price for you." Fighting back cynicism, I responded, "On the morning train from Madras," and shook his hand. There was something intriguing about him. He had an aristocratic demeanor.

"I know you tourists tire of Indian people, how do you say it, coming on strong at first," he said, "but it is our way. We want to make you feel at home."

Oh, sure, I thought, and then you want to take us to a very great artist who is your friend and who paints beautiful pictures. "We're rather tired right now," I said, "and just want to stretch our legs, explore your city. It looks fascinating."

"Allow me, sir and madam, to take you in my car. I will give you a wonderful tour of the city and then we can all go to my club for dinner."

I was taken aback by this, knowing that few Indians own their own cars.

Our new friend spoke mostly to Elaine, a switch from previous encounters in which men studiously ignored her in conversation. Perhaps Sikhs were a different breed. I hadn't actually met any until now, having not yet explored the north of the country where most of them reside.

Elaine had said, "Why not?" So we accepted the Sikh's offer and headed for his car. I thought Elaine had been somewhat taken in by the guy's charm. I explained on the way that we had no money to spend on anything but essentials. The Sikh laughed and said, "Of course not. I understand exactly. You are, how do you say it, budget travellers." He opened the door of an expensive-looking Opel.

A well-to-do resident of Calcutta—a rare breed in itself in this city of about twelve million people—might have many motives in capturing two tourists in a restaurant and chauffeuring them about town. One might be simply a yearning to talk to foreigners, and nothing else. I decided to give our friendly Sikh the benefit of the doubt.

Talk, he did—non-stop—as he showed us the intriguing sites. He was anything but boring. We saw unimaginable squalour practically alongside outlandish luxury; teeming masses sleeping outside the railway station, all their worldly goods in a paper bag; Hilton-like hotels in the downtown area; colonial buildings from the period of the British Raj; jam-packed, leaning buses spouting clouds of black smoke into the air; the occasional Mercedes, probably carrying some movie star to the studio (Calcutta is the centre of the Indian film industry, the biggest in the world). We saw snake charmers, grotesquely malformed beggars, society ladies decked out in colourful saris for afternoon tea, and even two bodies of those too poor for cremation services floating down the river. We saw what seemed like dozens of temples, mosques, a few churches, cinemas on every street and hundreds of man-pulled rickshaws, used as taxis. And, oh yes, in this throbbing city of so many millions, we counted exactly two traffic lights!

Four hours later, the car pulled up in front of Namur's club. It appeared opulent and very British-like, with a slightly dilapidated statue of Queen Victoria on the lawn, a reminder of a bygone day. A doorman greeted our host and parked the car. Namur smiled at us, as if to say, "See?"

We had drinks in the garden. It was all very bizarre, after the sights of the day. But then, in this land of paradoxes, it was easy to adapt to. I felt for a moment like a Mogul Prince, or like Lord Mountbatten being wined and dined before discussions of the British evacuation in 1947. Only Mahatma Ghandi was missing.

We dined lavishly. India has one of the world's greatest cuisines and plates of exotic fare appeared and disappeared as if by magic while we gorged ourselves. Only occasionally did I wonder, "Why is he doing this?"

I had an inkling as I noticed his continual flattery of Elaine. He would constantly look her up and down, commenting on everything from her voice, to her laugh, to her hair, to her Ukrainian ancestry, to her clothes. She, I noticed, was enjoying it all very much.

Was I being unfair? It was silly to be jealous of a Sikh who had to be fifty-five years old, or more. I convinced myself that Namur was just trying to make her feel at home and that, after dinner, Elaine and I would thank him profusely for a wonderful day, a tour of Calcutta par excellence, and be on our way.

Only then did it dawn on me that we hadn't even thought to find a room for the night. Oh well, no matter, we had found hotels before at ten at night.

As we were about to leave, Namur threw the bombshell. Turning to Elaine and taking her hand in his, he said, "I would be honoured if you would accompany me, as my escort, to a fashion show tomorrow evening at the Hotel Oberon. I know Jim would not be interested, but I am involved in the fashion industry, and I know you would be fascinated. All of Calcutta society will be there—movie stars, television people and prominent politicians."

I was about to protest when Elaine's eyes lit up. She said, "I would like that."

I felt myself redden, but turned to the Sikh and said, "Looks as though you have yourself a date!"

Namur dropped us at a hotel where we got a room. As he left he added, "A driver will drop Elaine's gown off tomorrow morning." He smiled at us both, waved and drove off.

"God, Elaine," I said, "He wants to show you off."

"I think he's nice," she responded, "and even cute." She laughed, seeing my jealousy. She kissed me and I realized I was being silly.

"I hope that is all he expects," I added.

I was embarrassed, showing the possessive side of me I thought I had conquered years before. Nothing more was said of it.

Our stomachs full, we tumbled into bed.

We spent the next day touring Calcutta by foot, stopping at outdoor markets laden with fruits and vegetables we could not even identify by name, but which we had both come to love during our travels in India. We bought ice cream from a man who made it from scratch, on the spot. I had a shave sitting on a stool in the street; Elaine got her hair trimmed.

We strolled beside the misty, almost ethereal, Houghly River and walked through the Maidan, an enormous park in the city centre, happy to have a short respite from the noise and the heat of the throbbing city.

When we returned to the hotel, Elaine's dress was waiting, thanks to Namur's driver. So was an enormous bouquet of flowers.

So far on this magical day, neither of us had mentioned Elaine's date for the evening.

"Why are you doing this?" I asked, as casually as I could, watching her try on the gown, noting how its style was provocative and accentuated her figure.

"Because I want to," she said, adding, "and because we left Canada to experience India. Is this not a good way to do so? Going to a fashion show with a charming man and meeting real Indian people."

"Yes, I agree," I said, fighting my jealousy, but admiring her gutsiness.

When she left with Namur, I took a stroll through the streets of Calcutta, had a leisurely meal in a little outdoor café and lined up for a movie ticket.

Indians are probably the most avid movie-goers in the world. Every showing is like a rock concert in America. People wait for hours. A guy wanting to impress his girl just naturally tries to get tickets for the latest hit film. More often than not, the movie would be made in India, but today the film was a James Bond thriller, which happened to have been shot in Udaipur, a city in Rajasthan where we had spent some time a few weeks before.

I have little recollection of the film itself. The real attraction was the audience at that large downtown cinema. The people came early, milled about the lobby, seemingly showing off their attire. Many of the movie-goers wore Western-style jeans, an anomaly in India. They checked one another out carefully, as patrons of a fashionable singles bar in Toronto might do. They bought beer and partied until the film started.

When the lights went down, they savoured the scenes containing violence and sex, watched intently, laughed in unlikely places and went for more beer and snacks during the scenes with even a little talk.

Before the credits rolled at the film's end, most of the crowd was gone in a flash. After the stampede, I lingered on the street in front of the cinema. It was like a carnival with food and drink sellers, people hawking wares—jewelry, clothes, crafts—musicians playing for a few pennies and rickshaw drivers fighting over fares.

I returned to the hotel about eleven, flopped on the bed and went to sleep. Only when I awoke about two a.m. and found no Elaine beside me did I give any thought to the fact that she might have been in any danger on her date with Namur.

I knew she was a woman who could fend for herself. I didn't fully understand her wanting to spend the evening with a Sikh she had known for less than twenty-four hours, but it was her mysteriousness that I found attractive. I accepted that in her, just as I doted on her other qualities: her warmth, her sense of humour, her open-mindedness.

For all I knew, Indian fashion shows ran late. Maybe she had gone to a post-show party. Maybe Namur was even more of a charmer than I had thought. Perhaps she had met other travellers and had gone out on the town with them.

I went back to sleep, waking every hour for the next three as I became increasingly worried. When daylight came, I was extremely upset. I frantically checked the hotel desk for messages.

There were none.

I went for coffee. When I returned to our room, I was astounded to find the police rummaging through my things, and Elaine's.

I doubt any police in the world are as officious as Indian police. They practically ignored me. I was flabbergasted.

Finally the one in charge spoke. "Miss Mochula has been arrested. We are looking for more evidence."

"Arrested? Evidence?" I gasped. "What do you mean?

"Hashish," the officer stated. "You are very lucky we found none in this room."

Shock and disbelief must have shown on my face. The cop added, "You should choose your friends more wisely."

I didn't ask any more questions. I got the address of the jail she was in and went directly by rickshaw.

Elaine was distraught when I got there. She said that she'd gone with Namur to a house party after the show, just for a drink, before heading back to the hotel. Hashish had been the drug of choice at the party. She had refused a couple of offers to join in. She'd also fended off Namur's sexual advances and was plotting some safe way of escaping the scene when the police entered the picture.

Angry, Namur, obviously wealthy and well-connected, had decided to play hardball. He simply called a crony in the upper echelons of the Calcutta police department and had Elaine jailed for hashish possession. We had heard stories about the corruption of Indian police forces, but had never dreamed we'd experience anything first-hand.

I wondered what the best move would be. Call the Canadian Embassy in Delhi? I conjured up a headline: "Canadian Woman Sentenced to 10 Years for Drug Trafficking."

Suddenly, a Sikh, who was obviously the police strong-armed interrogator, appeared.

Before I could offer any protests, the officer said, "You are very lucky, Miss. It has been explained to me that you were wrongly accused. You are to be released immediately."

Both Elaine and I were too stunned to say anything. We left the jail feeling numbed.

Namur had certainly vented his frustration over being turned down. His hospitality had obviously come with a price tag.

I looked at Elaine, puffy-eyed and recalled her telling me that she wanted to experience "all India has to offer."

As we lined up for train tickets to Kathmandu, she said, "Sure, I made a mistake, but it certainly beats sitting home in Ottawa watching television!"

That's the attitude a traveller has to have.

Stopping to Replenish the Bank Account

After travelling for three months in India and Nepal, we returned to Canada and, aware of the sorry state of my bank balance, I immediately set out to look for something I had put on the backburner long enough—work. I had to find some way of earning a living.

There had been many things I disliked about teaching. However, one aspect of the job I treasured was its holiday time. And it was never a nine-to-five job. So I knew that I did not want to become a clock puncher. I was not afraid of hard work, but I wanted to do it on my own terms, and not for twelve months a year. The idea of being a slave was ludicrous, for whatever kind of money.

I did not see work as anything approaching holiness and, yet, I wanted something satisfying. I didn't want to prostitute myself; life was too short. Did work make us better people? Did a little structure make getting through the day easier? I had come to believe the answer to those questions was—no. Most days did not have enough hours for me. I wanted to find something interesting, and fairly lucrative.

Freelancing, I quickly realized, was the answer. But freelancing at what? What skills did I possess? What skills do ex-English teachers have? I felt I could write. I didn't want to sell insurance, or real estate. I had had some success in selling articles to the *Toronto Star* after my job as a sportswriter had ended. The problem with freelance journalism, however, is that most papers have more than enough writers on their regular staff to cover the scene. A freelancer, unless he is a Pierre Berton or a Margaret Atwood, is going to have most of his work sent back to him with a note like this: "Good article, but one of our guys just did one on this subject (or is going to do one)."

And so I wanted to avoid such shooting in the dark. Since I lived in Ottawa, I naturally thought of the federal government as a source of work. After all, the Nation's Capital is a virtual Paper City, jam-packed with offices churning out reports, periodicals, brochures. I decided to try to ride the gravy train. I would try to obtain contracts to do writing jobs, a specific number of days and/or dollars attached to each contract, and work at home.

I had previously learned that resumés are worth only the paper they're written on. This time I used the direct approach. I got business cards printed, photo-copied samples of previous work, and made the rounds of government offices. After a week or so of making fruitless calls—during which I was constantly assured that, "While we have no need of writing services now, we will certainly have in the near future. You will be hearing from us,"—I decided to use contacts. That is, indeed, the magic word in job hunting—contacts.

The trouble was I had very few. Teachers can spend a lifetime in a classroom and, at the end, find themselves with a depressing lack of contact with the outside world. In addition, my career as a regular journalist was so short that I had made few real contacts. And I had worked for a paper that no longer existed.

I remembered meeting a former student in a restaurant one evening. She was now an editor in some government department. We reminisced about grade nine English class, an astounding—to me—fifteen years before! I decided to pay her a visit. Was she not a contact?

I think her ego liked the idea of her former high school teacher coming to see her in her spacious office on the twentieth floor of an ultra-modern building overlooking the Ottawa River. And my ego didn't object in the slightest; I was after a job.

And I got one, amazingly fast, considering the usual government red tape. I carefully agreed to master "our unique style—it's kind of breezy," noting the seriousness with which Ann Baxter took her job. I fleetingly remembered her as a mini-skirted, fun-loving young woman with limited writing skills, but a girl I had liked for her spirit. In the Public Service, she had done "better" than she, or anyone else, would have predicted. She had found a home in Paper City. And I, it seemed, had found a home with her for $150 per day, with each article needing about five days' work.

I bought an answering machine. The Public Service Commission—that is, Ann—would call me whenever they needed an article done for their monthly magazine, called *Dialogue*, or their weekly newsletter, Update. When I returned from a tennis game, or a luncheon date, or a bicycle ride, I would often find 'work' on my machine.

I'd go down to Ann's office, get the details from her, agree on the number of days required for the job, come back home, make myself comfortable and get down to work.

It didn't take long to learn about the accepted standards of efficiency and work-load. I finished my first article in three days and delivered it to Ann's office.

"But, Jim," she protested, in a hushed voice, "this is a five-day job. You shouldn't be finished in three!"

I caught on immediately. The final two days were the 'gravy.'

"Jeez, Ann," I said quickly, "I know what you're saying, but I just wanted you to check my first draft. I'm sure I can finish in two more days."

I knew she liked her power. I decided to play by government rules: milk it for all it's worth.

As I left, she said, smiling coyly, "Let's have lunch sometime. We can hash over old times."

I thought this was hilarious. Old times, eh? Her English essay I had marked fifteen years ago? Her smile told me she had other things in mind. I had noted that, even minus the sixties' miniskirt, Ann looked very good indeed.

I took my first article for *Dialogue* home with me and placed it on my desk to sit for two days until I could submit it without embarrassing anyone by beating the deadline. It 'earned' an extra $300 as it sat on my desk. Could there be some basis for Public Service bashing, after all? If I had taken part in the scam on my first assignment, what were the 'regulars' up to?

There was something about the subject matter and the style of my initial piece which made me instantly cynical. Here is what it was about: I had to interview an Associate Deputy Minister in the Department of Regional Industrial Expansion; plot out her career path for readers; show the reasons for her meteoric rise to the top (she had been a housewife only ten years previously); capsulize her management philosophy, her department's aims and objectives; and outline her main contributions over the past year. I realized quickly that I was writing propaganda; drivel for managers in every government office across Canada to read, stuff to make them say, "Wow, If she can do it, so can I!" Or to chuck in their wastebaskets.

I had to fill the thing with such phrases as, "The motivating force has always been to enjoy my work and achieve results," and, "Throughout my career, several people were prepared to take a gamble on me and let me test and prove myself," and, "If people don't feel there's meaning in their job, then I'm not being a good manager."

I resorted to taping interviews with bureaucrats after this first experience, as trying to take notes, reporter-like, did not work. I couldn't understand, let alone remember, what they were saying.

The guidelines for style told me that I must always be positive, that I must keep my sentences short—and cliché-filled—and carefully insert quotes which attested to the rewards of government service. I was to be extremely careful about titles, job descriptions, and always double-check with the interviewee before going to press. I thought, wryly, of the freedom I had as an untried baseball writer to do my story for next day's paper. Here, I had to submit to a half-dozen editors before the magazine went to press, a magazine which I could envision no person with a modicum of intelligence reading.

And so, realizing the absurdity early in the game, I decided to put integrity aside, earn some money, and do the job as long as I could stand it. For a short while, it was actually fun.

The crunch came when Ann asked me to do an article, the title of which made me flinch: "Career Opportunities for Young People in the Public Service in a Downsizing Situation." Each previous assignment had been a frustrating exercise in familiarizing myself with the appropriate jargon; this one was no different. I had first to learn what downsizing meant! The recently-elected Conservative government had promised to shrink the manpower in the Public Service.

After I did a double-take—I mean, surely the article could say, simply, that there were no opportunities for youth; that since Affirmative Action Programs remained in effect during downsizing (note how adept I became at using the jargon), then the very notion of there being openings for young people was absurd when jobs for francophones, women, native peoples, visible minorities, and the disabled had to be found—I agreed to do the job. I entered the office of the Director General of Staffing for the Public Service of Canada, tape recorder in hand.

His office was as large as my apartment, thickly broadloomed, plant-laden and furnished extravagently with a monstrous desk, chesterfield and chairs, and tasteful Canadian objets d'art. He looked tanned and fit in his impeccable pinstripes. He shook my hand, quickly protesting that he was very busy and could only spare a few minutes, adding, however, that "*Dialogue* is a great little magazine," and that "you guys are really doing worthwhile things down there."

I resisted asking where "down there" referred to, realizing it was probably government talk for the workplace of underlings, of the real 'servants.'

Before I turned on my tape recorder and unleashed my opening question, the Director General made a lengthy phone call in which he discussed, in much detail, the colour to be used in a two-page memo that would be sent to all department employees, and a recent business trip to Halifax where he had been "treated like a king" by those Maritimers who were the "salt of the earth" and "really know how to take care of you."

Then the busy man let loose at my tape recorder, after commending me for my decision to use it. "One thing that really bugs me is being misquoted. No offence meant to you, but one time when I was over at Transport, years ago . . . ," and he digressed for another five minutes, my tape whirling feverishly.

What I got from this bureaucrat was: there were no opportunities for youth in the Public Service at this time or in the forseeable future because the government was intent on cutting jobs. But we couldn't say that. We had to, in the usual jargon-filled manner, circumvent the issue. We had to lie to our readers.

Of course, he did not use those words. Instead, he indulged in the most embarrassing use of obfuscation and gobbledegook that I have ever heard. He insisted that I write that "Under the parameters of the Public Service Commission, all efforts will be made, in this time of employment constraint and severe downsizing measures, to assure that consideration be given to all young people both within the public service and outside the public service so that their career goals will not be adversely affected. Staffing programs would be in effect to keep morale at the usual high level during this period of fiscal restraint."

"What the hell are you talking about?" I finally said, unable to indulge this idiot any longer.

"I beg your pardon," he gasped, taken aback.

"How, in God's sake, can you blatantly lie to people?" I asked, adding, "And what kind of a fool do you think I am to sit here and let you believe anything you're saying makes any sense?"

"Heavens," he said, "this is most disconcerting. They told me you were an intelligent, capable journalist."

"Well, I sized you up as an over-inflated bag of hot air the minute I walked in here," I said.

I left the office, my tape recorder still whirling on the coffee table. Ann could retrieve it from this officious bore. I knew I wouldn't be asked to do any more articles for *Dialogue*—or for any other government publication.

Still, I had gotten about six months out of them, replenished my bank account and had a different work experience. There are limits, though, when it comes to what you can put up with.

My Shit Detector had bleeped.

Why Travel?

"Why do you like to travel?" my friend, Peter, asked me over a beer one evening.

His question made me examine my reasons for regularly plotting escapes from home. I pondered it for a few moments and answered that I travel to experience as much of the world as I can, to meet different people and learn about how they live. In learning as much as I can about other ways of life, perhaps I can improve my own.

Also, when you're on the road, there are distractions and challenges which enable you to gain a perspective that life at home, with its routine and security, does not always afford. It becomes easier to leave behind the 'shoulds,' that are a significant part of day-to-day life, and to start every day 'fresh.' On the road, you're 'involved,' constantly stimulated. In such a state, it is easier to focus on what is relevant and what is not. 'Getting away' becomes, paradoxically, a way of 'getting in' to yourself.

In addition, I told my friend that I travel as part of my attempt to find 'my niche.' Since I quit my teaching job at the age of forty, I've put considerable effort into finding a way of fitting in. It's not that I am totally dissatisfied with my life in Canada, but I wonder if there is somewhere out there where life does not evolve around 'getting and spending' to quite the degree that it does here. Whether or not the answer can be found 'out there' remains to be seen. But if I don't at least look, then I'll never know.

I finished my answer to Peter's question by admitting that I travel to escape winter. I know that sounds very un-Canadian, but as much as I ski and skate and love the outdoors, there is no way I can embrace a winter that drags on relentlessly from October until May! Sometimes I think the main thing that differentiates me from my fellow Canadians is my adamant refusal to accept a lifestyle which revolves around the indoors. Even on a beautiful summer or fall evening, the most common sight that strikes me on my nightly walks is the glow emanating from practically every house window—that of the ubiquitous television set. Mainly though, I function better in warmer climates.

I don't know if my answer satisfied my friend's curiosity or not. He'd never been a traveller. I think he regarded it as frivolous, even foolhardy and dangerous. He felt one should save one's money and shore oneself against impending bad times.

I suggested that he read a book entitled, *A World of Villages*, by a young American named Brian Schwartz who, upon graduating from Yale Law School and landing a job with a prestigious New York law firm, decided to pass up a career opportunity and go travelling. He ended up spending six years on the road, really on a shoestring, in Africa and Asia. He recounts his experiences in an exceptional book, one passage of which stands out in my mind. It is from a chapter entitled "Down and Out in Abidjan." He'd run out of money and was living in a flophouse in the slums.

"The poverty was not half as bad as I had imagined. I could survive it. This simple bit of knowledge was, I realized, something precious and rare, and I wished I could share it with those men and women in America who waste their lives doing work they hate, fawning on bosses they secretly despise, building ramparts that turn into prisons, and, in the end, tombs—and all to avoid leading, to insure themselves against the smallest possibility of ever being forced to lead, a life that was not really worse than theirs."

Schwartz's words struck a chord in me. We build walls to protect ourselves from what we see as potential harm or evil, but, in so doing, we close ourselves off from experience. Travel is one of the best ways of keeping out of that death-in-life rut.

A Train Ride in Yugoslavia

We had battled mosquitoes all night in a Thessalonika hotel. Elaine had been ill for a week, having picked up a bug in Athens. It was raining. We hadn't eaten breakfast before boarding the train at six a.m. We had been hassled by thug-like passport control officials as we entered Yugoslavia about nine o'clock. All in all, we were at a low ebb.

Elaine slept as I tried, in vain, to get some food for us. We shared a compartment with four men who had said nothing to us, or each other, since the train left Greece. One of the men, burly with a black moustache, seemed to be eyeing Elaine with interest.

When she opened her eyes, he handed her some grapes. She accepted them with thanks. The man smiled at her, but said nothing.

Some time passed and he offered me some grapes, and soon some biscuits for both of us. He continued to look intently at Elaine. Finally, he said something in a language I could not identify. Then, out of the blue, one of his companions said, "I think the lady is feeling unwell."

We explained our plight, our new friends nodding with concern and sympathy, as they listened to the translation of the one who spoke English.

He said to us: "What do you expect on a Greek train! I know, it's horrible—no food, everything filthy, unfriendly people. We are anxious to get out of this country."

"Where are you headed?" I asked.

"Moscow," he answered.

Seeing my surprise, he added, "We have been representing our country at a trade show in Thessalonika for several weeks. Now, if we survive this train, we will be home in three days." He laughed easily, translated into Russian for his friends, and they joined in.

Upon learning we were Canadian, our translator exclaimed, "I love your country. I was in Montreal for the Olympic Games in '76. The French Canadian women—oo, la la!"

He then did what he was to do for the rest of our time together; he translated for all concerned.

The burly one with the black moustache, Georgio, had identified Elaine as having some Russian blood—correctly, as her ancestry is part Ukrainian—and as suffering at the time from a stomach disorder. "I knew right away you had travelled in Greece," he added, through Vladimir, our translator. "Their food is too greasy for even dogs."

I admit I was taken aback by the friendliness and generosity of the Russians. This was 1982. No one in the West had even heard the name Gorbachev yet, and I had never spoken to a 'real Russian' before. I suppose I was prone to believing the American propaganda. Fresh in my mind were reports of their recent invasion of Afghanistan and I had been living in West Germany, several years before, when they had invaded Czechoslovakia. I had listened as President Kennedy called the Soviets' bluff in the Cuban Missile Crisis. So, all in all, Russians were the bad boys of the world. Why were these particular Russians everything they weren't supposed to be?

As we talked through Vladimir—he must have been exhausted—about things Russian and Canadian (food, cost of living, clothes, and, of course, hockey), one or the other of the Russians would disappear only to return with tea, served from a beautiful silver tea service, with delicious sandwiches, fruits of all kinds, and later, some great vodka—what else—and caviar!

"You mustn't be travelling light," I joked.

"Well, we like our Russian comforts," Vladimir told us. "Six weeks in Thessalonika. That is worse than, well, Siberia! We brought along trunks of food and drink."

"Especially drink," added Georgio, roaring with laughter.

And so for five hours, we were wined and dined in lavish style. Our hosts even straightened out our passport problems by calling for the conductor and scolding him harshly. They were cultured, civilized people—not upper-echelon Communist party members—just civil servants doing a job and anxious to get home. And no plane ticket home for them—only a slow train to Moscow.

I realized how lucky we were to have met them. Not so much because we were tired and hungry—and Elaine's sickness seemed to cure itself the minute we met them—but because the shibboleth of the cold, sinister Russian had been shattered. These Russians were friendly, caring, sophisticated and witty people.

We exchanged addresses. Georgio, whose home was in the Ukraine, was especially insistent that we visit, so that, "Elaine can meet her ancestors and eat some of my mother's perogies."

After handshakes and hugs on the platform of the Belgrade train station, we parted company. Never in our travels had we met more engaging people. The Soviet Union was now near the top of our 'Must Visit' list.

Our euphoria was to be short-lived. It was now midnight and pouring rain. The down side of travel suddenly entered the picture. We had to search for a room, tired as we were after partying all day!

We managed to change some money in the station and began our attempts to find out if there was a nearby budget hotel. We were immediately frustrated. We couldn't speak the local language and no one at the station knew any English. Still, we had faced this problem dozens of times on the road. It is just that our 'fall' from our pleasant train experience had been sudden and swift. Also, we had tried not to offend our hosts and had accepted one too many vodkas, perhaps.

Standing outside the station, we agreed on one thing: Belgrade was a dismal-looking place. People we approached for directions were unfriendly, if not hostile, and we wished we had stayed on the train.

After an hour of fruitless queries, we had resigned ourselves to sleeping in the station and catching a train for Ljubljana in the morning. The prospect, however, depressed us greatly. Sleep in a train station is well-nigh impossible.

Suddenly, out of nowhere, a young man emerged.

"Hello," he said, "I could hear you asking about a room. It is possible I help you."

We expressed interest, to put it mildly, and, within a few minutes, our new acquaintance returned with an old woman who looked at us suspiciously. The two of them spoke rapidly. It seemed she was reluctant to take us.

"How long do you stay?" he asked.

We had long ago learned that many people do not like renting a room for one night only, and so I said, "Oh, we aren't sure yet, probably a few days."

This was followed by furious discussion. Our answer did not seem to have pleased the woman.

"She says you must leave by eight in the morning," our new translator said.

Bewildered, I said, "Fine, we just want a place to sleep. We're tired."

More discussion.

"Do you have dinners?" he asked next.

"Dinners?" Elaine and I looked at each other, perplexed. It was then one o'clock in the morning!

"You have dinners?" He repeated.

"No, we do not need dinner," I said. "We just want to sleep."

This answer caused much consternation on the part of the woman, who shook her head vehemently when told what I had said.

A repetition of this exchange went on for five minutes or so. Finally, the young man said, "You have dinners. I saw you change money in the station."

Then it hit me! The topic under discussion hadn't been dinners, rather dinars, the Yugoslavian currency. Elaine and I broke out in laughter. I explained our faux pas to the guy, who relayed the explanation to the harried old lady.

She seemed not to appreciate the joke, but was relieved to find we had local currency and agreed to take us in. It seems that had we paid her in, say, U.S. dollars, she could be in real trouble, it being unlawful for her to possess them.

We paid upfront, in dinars, for the room and were told by our translator to follow the woman.

The rain had lessened somewhat, but the night was dark and cool. Belgrade slept as we followed the old lady through narrow, winding streets. She never once looked at us. It was a bit eerie.

Finally, after walking for about ten minutes, we came to an ugly highrise which we entered. As we climbed the stairs, I noted a faint smell of urine and a general rundown appearance. We trudged to the sixth floor. There was hardly any lighting in the hallway—about what you'd get from a twenty-five watt bulb.

We were let into her apartment—again virtually in darkness—and admonished to take off our shoes. We did as we were told.

The old woman immediately got an alarm clock and there, in the almost-darkness, set it for eight o'clock, once again reminding us we had to leave by that hour. We were too tired to argue.

Through another door, we followed our reluctant hostess. She pointed to what seemed to be two beds, or couches. The only light in this room was a dim nightlight. We could see nothing but the beds. They looked inviting.

After pointing at the clock once more, the old woman left us. Strange surroundings notwithstanding, we fell asleep at once.

The alarm went off on schedule. I opened my eyes. What I saw in the now-bright room astonished me. Elaine noticed too. We gasped, "The kitchen!"

We had been charged hotel prices to sleep in the kitchen of a poor woman's apartment! So that was the reason for the fuss—she wanted us out so she could cook her breakfast.

She did not offer us any, as she hastily bade us goodbye.

Call it East Block entrepreneurism. We later learned that many elderly people in countries with no social security are forced to double as undercover guesthouse operators. We were then more forgiving in our thoughts about the grouchy old woman. She was just making a living.

Still, as the rain continued to come down, we were not unhappy to be on the train once more, leaving dreary Belgrade behind us, dinars and all. Maybe we'd be fortunate enough to run into more Russians!

Albert and Miss Gwynne— A Jamaica Welcome

There are compensations when you just cannot find that second career and opt instead to take to the road.

I've met people while travelling who will be lifelong friends.

Of course, you can meet interesting, imaginative people right at home too. The problem is you often don't. Careers, social obligations, and the hectic pace of life all tend to get in the way. On the road, I have found people to be generally more open to, well, just stopping to chat. Other travellers, certainly, are usually starving for conversation and local people, particularly in Third World countries, are eager to meet foreigners. Time seems to mean nothing to them. Perhaps it is the absence of technological diversions which makes for enhanced practice of the art of conversation—or maybe it is just the lack of anything else to do.

Albert and his wife, Miss Gwynne, Jamaican friends I have stayed with on four different occasions, are two people who made a difference in my life as a traveller.

I had wandered into their yard on my first trip to Jamaica, desperate to get out of the ninety-five-degree heat, having just arrived from Canada where it had been minus twenty degrees. I had craved for the heat and sun, but not quite so fast. I was wilting, and frustrated at being unable to find any accommodation.

An elderly man and woman were sitting on the porch in the shade with a small, black dog at the man's feet. It was too hot for the dog to react. Indeed, the man seemed asleep, his head sagging while the woman greeted me with a simple, "Hello, man, what you want?"

"Do you know where I can find a room?"

She laughed. "Of course. I have room right here. You go inside, take a look. My, my, but you look hot!"

I liked the room, just off the porch, and was even more pleased when the lady, who said her name was Miss Gwynne, presented me with a cold glass of juice.

"You like soursop?" she asked. "Good for you, man. Cool your tummy," and she smiled and rubbed her stomach.

She disappeared and I sat on the porch, next to the old man, to enjoy the tropical fruit drink. It was the first of many exotic delicacies I was to sample sitting in that chair.

The old man eventually woke up. "Good to have you here, man," he said. "Albert and Miss Gwynne look after you good."

I thanked him for taking me in, noticing that he appeared to be older than his wife, and very thin, almost frail.

He pointed to the sleeping dog. "Blackie," he said, "he keep out thieves. He protect people like you. You no worry. Everything be cool for you, man."

I noted his phrase, "People like you," and I knew he meant white tourists when he squeezed the black skin on his thin arm and said, "Blackie know who to bark at. He never bark at people like you. He keep out thieves."

"He's a good watchdog," I said.

"Yes, man," said Albert, laughing, slapping his knee. "Blackie good watchdog. That's it. Yeah, man—watchdog."

"You have a beautiful place here," I said, noting how the porch faced the ocean a hundred yards or so away. I could feel the cooling breezes already.

"Is it so?" Albert said, feeling complimented. "Is it so?" he repeated as if he doubted I really felt that way. "Well, we just want you people to be happy." He added, as I later found he would always, for emphasis, "Be happy, man."

Albert then offered me a drink of white, overproof rum, the first of many I would have with him on the porch in Negril. Some would characterize him as a hopeless alcoholic; I do not. Rather, I see his drinking as part of his retirement lifestyle. He had earned the right to please himself in the last years of his life.

Albert had been a cook on a Jamaican freighter in his youth, had sailed the Caribbean until he was forty, never having a home, always away from his family. He had then gotten a break: he went to Manchester, England, where he spent about twenty-five years as a welder in a factory. Some break! He worked for two years in Manchester before he could afford to have Miss Gwynne join him (Jamaican married women over the age of fifty are referred to as Miss). They had made trips home to visit relatives only twice during their time in England. A few years before I first met them, they had returned to Jamaica with a small pension. Like many retired people the world over, they put in time: Albert sitting on the porch, looking at the sea he had missed so much in Manchester; Miss Gwynne looking after Albert, going to the market, attending church. They took in the occasional tourist to make ends meet.

I came to regard their little house as a home away from home and looked forward to talking with Albert on the porch in the cool of the evening. Drinks in hand, my body pleasantly burning from the day's sun, we would watch the comings and goings on the road between the house and the sea, Miss Gwynne commenting periodically from her room just off the porch, missing nothing as she slowly shelled peas from the garden.

Not a night went by without Albert saying, slapping his leg in glee, "By gosh, man, I think it be cold in England now," adding, "Sure glad I not there any more," with a wistfulness that belied his words.

England might have been cold, but Albert had been young then, and active. He would often badger Miss Gwynne into getting out the photo album to show me pictures of the two of them dressed up "ready to go dancin', man." And they were, indeed, a handsome couple, Albert rakish in a double-breasted striped suit and fedora, gold-chained pocket watch glistening along with his then-perfect white teeth.

One night, shortly after my arrival, I sat with Albert on the porch, listening to yet another tale from his past. Out of nowhere came a grotesque-looking human being. Blackie, true to his training, barked ferociously. Albert yelled, "Sic him, Blackie, sic him," and became more agitated than I had ever seen him.

I could make out the figure and face of a man dressed in rags, literally, with a crazed look in his eyes. He was clearly frightened, though at well over six feet and with only Blackie to deal with, he needn't have been.

The intruder went around to the back of the house, letting out a piercing, anguished wail as he passed the porch. In the moonlight, I thought he looked about middle-aged, and as wild as if he'd just emerged from years in the jungle.

Albert settled down, sipped his rum and was silent. He closed his eyes as he often did at this hour and might have dozed off. I noticed my hand was shaking as I picked up my drink.

I could hear Miss Gwynne talking to the crazed man at the back. She seemed to be feeding him. The sounds of him eating were animal-like, full of satisfaction. Miss Gwynne spoke in the patois of the island and I could make little sense of it. The man grunted and slurped contentedly.

Within ten minutes, the feeding over, the visitor stormed off. Blackie barked ferociously again. Albert quickly woke up, shouting encouragement to the dog as before. "Get him, Blackie!" he yelled, spilling his precious overproof as he leaped from his chair.

"What's going on, Albert?" I asked.

"That man no good," he said. "He not welcome here. He bad man, like animal. You people not like him. You not come to us if he be here."

I decided not to press him. I was bewildered. Within a half hour, though, all was back to normal. It was another perfect night in Negril.

The next day, I broached the subject of last night's visitor with Miss Gwynne in the kitchen. Albert was still sleeping, as usual, though it was ten o'clock.

"Oh, yes," sighed Miss Gwynne, "that poor man Albert's son."

"His son!"

"He born like that, long before I know Albert. Albert look after him for forty years now. Always send money from England. Somebody always feed him." She sighed again, saying, "We not to question why God do things."

Albert's pathetic son made several appearances during my times with them. Albert always received him in the same way.

I am happy to report that Albert's son was, miraculously, 'cured' of his disease a few years later. In desperation, Miss Gwynne had taken him to the local clinic where a doctor, instead of telling them to go away, as had happened countless times in the past, had prescribed a drug to help control his disorder. The man was suffering from schizophrenia, something that would likely have been discovered and treated in early childhood in Canada.

Life with Hugh and Helen

It seems every time I travelled to Jamaica, I wandered into somebody's yard and ended up staying for weeks.

This time, on another trip, Elaine and I had rented bicycles one day to find a place to stay. In the tropical sun, a bike cuts down on the number of hours you have to spend under the blistering rays, wonderful as they may be in moderation.

The house we approached was as luxurious and spacious as Albert and Miss Gwynne's was simple and small. A man sat in a chair on the verandah, an iron grill creating a prison-like effect. I stuck my face against the bars.

To my greeting and query, the man grunted lazily, "Who sent you here?"

"Ingrid," I answered. "We met her on the minibus from Savannah-La-Mar and she told us she rented a room around here. I don't know if this is the place or not."

I seemed to have said the magic word, for the man, who appeared to be in his late twenties, got up and called, "Helen, Helen, come here. Ingrid send these people to us."

Helen emerged from inside. She was beautiful, looking very un-motherly in her slinky dress that left little to the imagination. Her three little daughters trailed after her, the youngest barely walking, the oldest about six. She smiled, opened the iron gates and said, "Ingrid, she sure get around," and laughed, amused at something.

"Do you rent rooms?" I said, speaking to both Helen and the man I assumed to be her husband.

"It's up to Hugh," she said.

When we looked at the size of the house, we wondered why a man of such means would be renting rooms. Hugh seemed reluctant.

"How long you stay, man?" he mumbled. He seemed groggy, out of it.

"I don't know," I said. "A couple of weeks, probably."

"I only rent room by the month," he said.

Strange, I thought. "OK, how much?" I asked.

Hugh squirmed in his chair, rubbed his head with his hand, saying, "I don't usually do this, man," rubbing his head again, adding, "I party last night, tired today. Tomorrow we talk about price."

That suited us fine. We'd have a night to see how we liked the place. Hugh was not exactly a welcoming host. Helen, though, seemed pleased we were staying and offered us cold beer. We sat with them on the verandah, looking at the world outside through the iron grill.

The barricaded house did not surprise us too much. We had discovered that Jamaicans are manic about thieves: the 'haves' protect their property. This young couple obviously had something to protect. I wondered what Hugh was involved in. Besides tourism, there wasn't much to work at in Negril.

An hour after we arrived, a motorcycle roared into the yard. A Jamaican with flowing dreadlocks was driving with a blond on the back. We recognized the woman at once as Ingrid.

"Hey, man," she exclaimed, seeing us on the verandah. "You found the place!" She walked up to the gate, hair dripping wet. I remembered, from our brief meeting on the bus, that she had come to the island from West Germany three months before, and had met and fallen in love with a Jamaican. She told us she was trying to earn a living here by escorting German tour groups around the island. She said she would be staying in Negril "forever, man."

In her swimsuit, Ingrid looked extremely well-endowed. I couldn't help thinking of how Jamaican men like their women to be, well, perhaps not fat, but substantial. I also knew that many of them were attracted to white women. Ingrid, with her blond hair and fair skin, filled the bill perfectly.

The driver did not stay, roaring off immediately. Ingrid had obviously just hitched a ride.

As Helen and Ingrid talked, I could tell Helen envied her guest's freedom. And she resented the way the local men fawned after this white-skinned woman. Still, the two were friends and talked constantly. Hugh dozed a while, getting up to leave as the kids became more and more rambunctious. Jamaican men are not noted for dedication to the family. Hugh went off to the neighbourhood bar.

When Helen was putting the girls to bed, Ingrid emerged from her bedroom. Her dress almost made me gasp. She was dressed as if she were going to the opera in Hamburg. She wore a long black outfit, lowcut in front, with high heels and an array of jewelry that was dazzling.

She sat in the chair beside us and lit a cigarette, looking at her watch. "Sonny's late again," she said. "Jamaican men are never on time."

"Is that the fellow who owns the water sport business?" Elaine asked, recalling his name plastered on billboards near the beach. He took tourists boating, water skiing and scuba diving.

"Yes, the same," she said. "What a guy he is, what a great guy." She took a long, satisfying drag on her cigarette. "I never knew such a man in Germany. And I never expected to fall in love again."

Ingrid had a hardness about her, yet she seemed genuine. Her candor was disarming.

"Sonny is a great lover," she smiled, "and he knows how to make money. He introduced me to lots of people, the right kind of people," and she gave us a knowing look.

I didn't know what she meant, but believed she was referring to connections for getting tour guide jobs.

"This is a tough country to make it in," she said, adding, "and I intend to make it. I want never to return to Europe. This place has got the vibe, man!"

I liked her German-accented 'Rasta talk.' Street-smart, there was still a 'little girl' vulnerability about Ingrid.

Without warning, after looking at her watch, she bolted from the verandah, and was off into the night, saying, "Ciao."

In a few minutes, Helen joined us. Hugh had not returned for dinner, but Helen made no reference to his absence. She seemed fascinated by her blond house guest, talking constantly about her clothes, the number of pairs of shoes she had, the way she would leave on the spur of the moment, go to Kingston for a week and return with exciting stories to tell. Still, Helen said she worried for Ingrid's safety.

"She goin' to find trouble," Helen said. "She fool around with Sonny and he married. Jamaican woman not take it sittin' down."

She went on to tell us about how she dealt with Hugh's occasional infidelities. As I looked at Helen's beautiful body in the moonlight, I wondered why Hugh would need to stray. I knew Jamaican men were macho, but to cheat on a woman like Helen . . .

"Hugh fool around last year with Jenny's daughter," she went on, referring to a woman down the road who ran a bakery which she staffed with three attractive daughters. "I find out about it. I wait up for Hugh one night. When he come back, I throw brick through car windshield. He cut bad, have to go to hospital, but he learn lesson: he don't fool around no more."

Seeing our shock, she laughed, "You look surprised. I tell you the truth—Jamaican women have to look after themselves."

After a while, Hugh came up to the gates and Helen let him in with her key. I was still perplexed by the elaborate security and longed for the openness of Albert and Miss Gwynne's porch. There was little breeze here. I decided to take a walk after Hugh had entered, mumbled a hello and went off to bed.

It struck me as I walked down the road, looking up at the clear sky filled with a thousand stars, that twelve hours had passed since we cycled into Hugh and Helen's yard and we had been too occupied, too stimulated by all the activity, to bother returning the bikes we had rented. Oh, well, we'd return them tomorrow. In Jamaica, everything "soon come."

Instead of two weeks, we stayed almost two months at Helen and Hugh's house. Not once in that period did a day go by that lacked activity of some sort—be it amusing, frustrating, even exciting. Routine in paradise? Lazy days in the sun? Quiet nights on the porch? Nothing to do but read? Not at Helen and Hugh's.

We became part of their world. In talks with Helen, often over breakfast, the littlest child climbing over me, fascinated by the odd-looking white man, I received a crash lesson in Jamaican customs and attitudes. She spoke of the large family she came from, nine children in all, and how her father became a successful owner of a fleet of taxis. Indeed, I sometimes saw him in town, driving a brand new Toyota. Helen pointed out that the key to her father's success was his abstaining from alcohol and drugs, a rarity among Jamaican men.

"I don't use drugs," said Helen, adding, "but if other people use them, it don't bother me," likely suspecting that, like most tourists, we occasionally used the ubiquitous Jamaican marijuana, or ganja. "I see too many lives ruined here."

She liked to question us about life in Canada. Helen assumed we were from the United States. She considered Canada part and parcel of America. Like most Jamaicans, she assumed everybody in America was rich. I gave up trying to explain that we were not rich, that we did not own a big house and two cars. I might have saved my breath: We were there, weren't we? We paid our rent, didn't we?

I was intrigued. Helen lamented their lack of money constantly, yet, here we were, in a house which only people well-to-do could afford. And Hugh constantly lounging around, sleeping until noon every day. Helen's only statement about him was, "Things not going too well for Hugh these days."

Sometimes during the night, I could hear Hugh talking to visitors. Odd, perhaps, in Canada, but not out of the ordinary here, where it isn't unusual to hear music blaring from a ghetto blaster or people partying well into the night.

Still, the night callers would stay for only a few minutes and then roar off by car or motorcycle. There seemed to be no pattern to it.

Then again, Hugh would disappear for three or four days, and Helen would only say, "Hugh have some business in Montego Bay," or wherever, and seem reluctant to talk about it. I wondered if, perhaps, he had a girlfriend, but discounted that idea when I thought of Helen's rock through the windshield.

Another odd thing: Hugh would occasionally try to borrow money from me, saying, "Just a little 'small,' man. I'm short, and the kids need food." This, after I had just paid a month's rent the previous day. He would assure me I could just deduct the 'small' from my next rent payment. I usually refused him the loan.

One night we were awakened by a loud banging on the iron grill. It went on for a few minutes and I heard, "Hughie, open up. We know you're in there, you bastard."

No answer from Hugh. The banging continued.

We lay in bed. These visitors sounded dangerous. I felt for Helen and the kids. Still, there was no sound from their rooms.

After much banging, the callers left, yelling, "We'll be back, you little blood clot."

Blood clot—the ultimate insult in Jamaican profanity. I suspected Hugh owed these men money.

The next morning, though, Helen offered no information and played down the racket. "They were drunk," she said.

Now we guessed the reason for the iron barricades. Jamaica has a lucrative drug trade. Hugh had to be involved in it at some level. Life went on.

Ingrid came and went, almost like a phantom. Sometimes she would come in about six in the morning, just as we were beginning to stir. Then again, she might come in around the dinner hour, have a nap and be off again. Or she would go on "a little trip," and return in a week's time.

I managed to have a few conversations with her. One time, after breakfast— she had, surprisingly, gone to bed early the previous night—we sat in the shade of a grapefruit tree out back, drinking coffee. She talked about her life in Hamburg. As far as I could make out, she had been a waitress, or possibly a go-go dancer, though she didn't use that term. Mostly, she talked about "all the different kinds of people I have met." There was the guy from Martinique: "Very rich. He was so kind to me." And the American, from New York: "He played in a reggae band. Oh, he could play!"

Then, in what I thought was a non sequitur, "I have had many men," she said, "but I do not sleep with any man I do not like." She then bolted to her room because, "Sonny is picking me up. He is driving me to the airport in Montego Bay. I am going to Bahamas for the weekend."

Bahamas for the weekend! Not your usual excursion from Negril.

Helen filled me in after Sonny and Ingrid left. It seems an old friend of Ingrid's invited her to come to the Bahamas, all expenses paid. A German, he liked to gamble in the casinos there. I thought of Sonny, the man she supposedly loved. Perhaps, Ingrid, too, liked to gamble, in a different way.

"How does Sonny feel about this?" I asked.

"Ingrid have right to take her opportunity," she said. "If I get the chance, I do it too."

"So Sonny doesn't mind?"

"Sonny not own her," Helen said. "Sonny knows Ingrid must make money. Not only that, Jim, what become of Ingrid when Sonny tire of her?"

I admired the clear line of demarcation between love and business. This was a country in which money did not come easily. Neither Sonny nor Helen were hung up on romantic concepts of love.

Helen then said something which floored me. "I wish I had sugar daddy."

"What?" I said.

"I want man to spend money on me," she said, matter-of-factly. "I know I have what men want. Jamaican men want it for nothing. But I think, in America, men pay for it. Is it so, Jim?"

I knew Helen wasn't coming on to me. We had become friends and she must have known I considered her attractive. But she surely knew I wasn't rich, and I was living there in the same room as Elaine.

She went on. "I want to find a man and go to America. I hear Florida is wonderful. There are many rich men there."

"I doubt you'd like Florida much, Helen," I said. "It lacks the beauty of Negril."

She interrupted me, seemingly lost in her fantasy. "I want no more children from Hugh," she said, and left to attend to one of her daughters.

I sat under the mango tree and pondered the lives of these two women with whom we were sharing the house. Ingrid and Helen, so different on the surface, had more in common than it seemed: both seemed intent on surviving in a world that undervalued them. They were, in effect, thumbing their noses at it. Ingrid was out there in the marketplace; Helen was planning her entry into it.

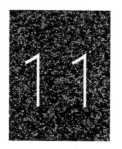

Not So Peaceful in Paradise

Ingrid returned from the Bahamas. Sonny visited her often, spending nights occasionally. Hugh continued to lounge around the house, sometimes having late-night callers, always trying to get advances on his rent money. Helen liked to talk—whenever she had a moment from caring for the children, shopping, cooking, doing laundry—and proved to be a bountiful source of local culture, history and gossip.

We filled our days exploring, swimming, reading, writing and eating wonderful seafood lunches, always followed by a short siesta. We'd often shop for fruit and vegetables in the market and managed to make some local friends. But it was the evenings at the house that Elaine and I most looked forward to.

One night, as we walked into the yard after eating out, we were startled to see a police jeep out front. I heard one of the little girls crying loudly and hurried to open the gate. Hugh was being roughly held against the wall by a burly cop, Helen screaming at the officer in the Jamaican patois.

Seeing us, the other policeman said, "Who are you? What do you want here?"

Helen yelled again. I could tell she was informing the police that we, indeed, lived there.

"Where is your room?"

I pointed in the direction of our bedroom. One cop immediately ordered me to unlock the door. I told him there was no lock on the door. He seemed surprised.

Entering my room, he demanded our passports. When he checked them out, he proceeded to rifle through our belongings. I had heard stories of Jamaican police and their brusque ways and decided to say nothing.

Now, instead of Hugh, who was handcuffed to the iron trellis, I was the object of the cops' curiosity. After a few minutes, the one said to the other, "The man's clean."

"Clean?" I asked, bewildered.

The police ignored us and returned to Hugh, yelling at him, shoving him repeatedly against the iron bars. Two of the kids were now screaming and a small crowd of curious neighbours had gathered out front.

Hugh was taken away in the jeep. Helen had, surprisingly, calmed down.

We sat down in the kitchen, my knees wobbly.

"Hugh is so stupid, so stupid. He go get caught again. He promise me he not sell the stuff any more. He swear he not use it any more. He just a fuckin', no good, lazy liar."

She was now incensed.

"Cocaine?" I asked.

"Sure," said Helen. "Everybody using it now in Negril. Hugh got caught last year and he get off. My father hire good lawyer. The bastard—he promise me he quit it."

Some things started to add up now—the big house for one thing, Hugh's drowsy, washed-out behaviour for another. And the night-time visitors, and the out-of-town trips. I had always expected cocaine dealers to be tough, sinister-looking people; Hugh had looked so harmless, so indolent. I had just never met a junkie before.

"What's going to happen now, Helen?" Elaine asked.

"I hope they keep him in jail for good," she yelled, but then added, "but the girls . . ." She fell silent, trying to fight back tears.

Just then, Ingrid burst into the house.

"The police," she said. "They were here? Were they looking for me?"

Told about the fate of Hugh, she relaxed, seemed to catch herself and said to Helen, "God, that's terrible. Poor Hugh. Can your father pull some strings again?"

The two women talked for a few minutes, until a motorcycle pulled into the yard. Sonny came in the door. He often called on Ingrid after work. They would spend time in her room, then have a smoke or drink on the verandah and head off for their night on the town. Though their relationship had been going on for a couple of months now, they were very much like new lovers. They couldn't get enough of each other.

Brought up-to-date on the happenings, Sonny smiled coolly, shaking his head. "Hugh not very smart. Jesus, he shouldn't have started back so soon."

I found the casual acceptance of drug pushing a bit unsettling. Few condemned it on moral grounds. There was little talk in Jamaica about how cocaine can kill.

Sonny took Ingrid by the hand and led her to her room. Helen returned from putting the kids to bed and sat quietly beside us. The night was quiet. As we talked, I was conscious of the two lovers only a few feet away. Helen seemed to have put Hugh's arrest in the back of her mind and was busy telling us about tomorrow's episode of *Dynasty* which she and her girlfriends from across the road were going to watch—if the television reception was good enough.

Every Wednesday, the women would watch the soap opera, commenting constantly on the action. "She should leave the bastard!" one would shout. "No, man, he is too rich!" another would say. "Watch out, watch out! The son-of-a-bitch has a gun!" one of them would yell. I loved to watch with them. They, not *Dynasty*, were the entertainment!

After Sonny and Ingrid had been inside for about an hour, a car drove up. A woman got out, and came up to the house.

Very quietly, she said to Helen, "I want to see Sonny."

I could tell Helen was shocked. She said nothing, merely stared, wide-eyed at the woman.

"It's Sonny's wife," she whispered, as the woman made a bee-line for Ingrid's room, as if she knew the lie of the land.

I heard her open the unlocked door.

"Jesus, woman!" I heard Sonny gasp.

Then, there was a shot. We were all horrified, frozen to our chairs.

Ingrid screamed hysterically. "Oh, Sonny! Oh, Sonny! Oh, Sonny!"

Sonny's wife stormed out of the room, gun in hand. She seemed not to notice us on the verandah, got into her car and drove off.

Ingrid followed screaming. "He's dead, he's dead."

We ran to the bedroom. Sonny was unconscious, and there was a lot of blood on the sheets. We thought he'd been shot in the arm, near the shoulder. I had never seen a man shot before, but I had the feeling Sonny was not, as Ingrid feared, dead. Elaine took his pulse. It was strong, but he was losing a lot of blood.

I asked Helen for the keys to Hugh's car, praying the seldom-used car would start. It did.

I brought it to the front of the house and the four of us loaded Sonny into the back. We headed for the only doctor in town, hoping he'd be still at the local clinic.

Ingrid had calmed down, especially when Sonny regained consciousness and started to talk. He was in pain and he was scared. That made for five terrified people in a wreck of a car barrelling down Negril's only paved road to the clinic, about three miles away.

The doctor was, thankfully, on duty. He stopped Sonny's bleeding in a short time, gave him some painkillers and told him he'd be alright.

"His wife do this?" he asked Helen, barely disguising a disapproving glance at Ingrid.

Told she had, he added, "Lucky for Sonny, Jamaican women never shoot straight."

The rest of the evening was taken up by yet another police interrogation, the second that day for us. We were on a roll.

About midnight, Ingrid, Helen, Elaine and I sat on the verandah, drained.

Sonny recovered, though he gave up visiting Ingrid at the house. Hugh got out of jail again, after three weeks—something about lack of evidence (Helen's father had once again pulled some strings). Ingrid continued to dart around Jamaica; she seemed to get over Sonny after a couple of weeks of 'mourning.'

The mourning seemed to consist of constant partying, a good deal of daytime sleeping, early evening backgammon matches at a nearby cafe and, I suspected, a liberal use of various drugs.

Whenever Ingrid stopped for breath at the house, she talked non-stop about her whirlwind life, never mentioning the shooting incident except for a brief comment the morning after.

"Man, I was scared," she confided. "I thought the crazy woman was going to kill me." Later, she added, "It is not the first time a guy's wife has gone nuts over me."

"Did you ever expect anything like that though?" I asked her.

"I was worried, man. I know women. I told Sonny we should go to Montego Bay. He could have his business there. But he refused to go."

She seemed to be implying that he got what he deserved. Her coldness stunned me. Where had the love gone, I wondered?

Noticing my silence, Ingrid said, "Look, man, I was giving Sonny as much as he was giving me. He had a choice, man. He wouldn't leave that woman. He told me that one time, a few years ago, she took a knife to him. I tell you, the woman is crazy."

She then became bouncy and animated, as if she had just flipped a switch.

"Helen, Helen," she yelled, summoning her, excitedly. "Come here. I want to tell you about Black Uhuru."

Helen's eyes opened wide. Black Uhuru was the most popular reggae band in Jamaica at the time. Music is king on the island; reggae musicians are revered.

"I was with them last night, after their show," she said.

"Ingrid!" Helen shrieked. "You are joking."

"No, man, I met them at Rick's Café before the concert. Their lead guitarist challenged me to a backgammon game. He flipped when I put twenty dollars on it. I won, of course, and he invited me to attend the show as his guest." Since Helen was still bug-eyed, Ingrid added, "I spent the night at his hotel."

Helen shrieked again.

I wondered if the musician had a wife. If so, I hoped for Ingrid's sake she was far away.

Ingrid proceeded to give us a blow-by-blow—well, almost—account of the concert and the aftermath, seemingly inspired by Helen's vicarious interest, not to mention our own.

Helen would sigh, laugh, giggle in envy. Ingrid was in a groove.

"He asked me to go to Kingston tomorrow," she said, and added, matter-of-factly, "he has an apartment. It will be great fun."

Helen frowned, coming slightly down to earth. "You must be very careful in Kingston, Ingrid. It is dangerous, especially for you."

She was, no doubt, referring to her white skin, her blond hair, and the fact Kingston was renowned for violence—muggings, theft, rape.

"I can look out for myself," she stated. "Anyway, Black Uhuru are like Rolling Stones. Very famous. They love to party after the shows, man. They have everything. They go first class."

She was, indeed, her old self.

It was quiet without Ingrid. And nobody called on Hugh during the night. Even Helen's soap opera friends stopped coming on Wednesday nights. Christmas was approaching, as unlikely as it seemed in the tropical heat. One thing that served as a reminder was the constant blaring of Christmas music, always to the reggae beat. It became as irksome as the canned, shopping mall music back home. 'Jingle Bells,' 'I'm Dreaming of a White Christmas,' 'Silent Night'—and all to the reggae beat.

Ingrid did not return for Christmas. After she had been gone for three weeks, Helen stopped talking about her and the danger she was surely in. Not a word was heard from her. Only her room reminded us of her. I would look at the closed door and think of her clothes and shoes stashed there, wondering if she'd ever return to claim them.

Hugh began to complain about Ingrid's rent being in arrears and how he wanted to rent the room to get much-needed money. Helen always admonished him, "Be patient, she soon come back." Hugh was not in a position to argue. He realized he owed his freedom to Helen's father.

To say there was a lack of festive spirit would be an understatement. Still, Christmas with Helen and Hugh was memorable because of its simplicity. No tree. No gifts for the kids. (We did, however, buy a small gift for each of the children; they were ecstatic with their little rag dolls we had found in the market.)

Helen cooked a fine dinner of curried goat—Hugh actually joined in—and we all got pleasantly drunk on Jamaican wine. We had given the couple a bottle of their favourite drink, Tia Maria, and they insisted on sharing it with us.

I couldn't help thinking of the material excessiveness of Christmas in Canada. While I missed my daughters, I felt privileged to be sharing the occasion with my Jamaican friends. Although we had known them for only a couple of months, we felt a bond. I think they did, too—we had shared some dramatic moments together.

We left Negril a week later.

Only when we next returned, two years later, did we learn that Helen's anxiety about Ingrid, footloose in Kingston, was well-founded. She had been attacked with a knife by—you guessed it—the wife of a reggae musician, a woman who resented losing her guitar-playing man to a white girl from Germany. Helen told us Ingrid had gone back to Hamburg.

"She not get killed, but she not look pretty any more."

And Helen and Hugh? Hugh was nowhere to be seen the day we visited. I assumed he was sleeping off a late-nighter in the house—or I should say one of the two houses now gracing their property. They planned to rent out the new one, Helen told us. She also told us, matter-of-factly, "I'm pregnant again, but this is the last one, for sure."

From what did the family income derive? I didn't ask.

Running into Mr. T.

If there's any truth in the idea that one way of avoiding the pitfalls of so-called middle age is to land yourself in new environments, then a man I met one morning in Negril personifies taking that 'quantum leap.'

In tropical countries, I often go jogging in the early morning, about six-thirty, before it's too hot to even think about working out.

Normally, these morning runs have been uneventful. I savour the quiet in the streets before the onslaught begins and feel uplifted watching the sun peaking over the horizon as I jog along an ocean road or a mountain path.

One day, I was startled to find myself face-to-face with two snarling German Shepherds; they had malice in their eyes. I froze, wondering if there was any way out.

All of a sudden, a man's voice rang out, "Where the hell do you think you're going?"

"Just for a run," I answered, shakily.

"A run? What the fuck are you talking about? You're on my property."

Though I doubted the man's charge to be true, I resisted arguing.

"I'm sorry," I said. "I'm just getting a little exercise."

"Come over here," the voice demanded.

Approaching the man, who now had the dogs under control—I hoped—I saw that he was white, not Jamaican, and looked to be in his late forties, fit and tanned.

"You could get shot running around people's property," he said. "Nobody likes trespassers in Jamaica."

I could see now that he was playing a joke at my expense. The man's eyes twinkled and danced playfully as he spoke.

"People around here call me Mr. T.," he said, as we introduced ourselves.

"You're spending the winter here?" I asked.

"Ha! You could say that, I guess," he smiled, seemingly amused.

"How long you here for?" I said.

"A good long time, I hope. And I assume my wife and kids feel the same way."

Just then, a striking black teenager bolted out the door of the house I now noted to be impressively large, pausing only long enough to plant a kiss on the man's cheek. "Bye, Dad," she said, giving me a smile as she left.

I didn't think anything of this. A white man living with a black woman was not uncommon in Jamaica. Surrogate parenthood is a Caribbean fact of life.

"I got five more of 'em as well," the man said proudly, adding, "or at least it was at last count."

This guy's woman must be something special, I thought. He'd perhaps gotten more than he'd bargained for.

Another teenager, this one male, bounded out of the house, and got into one of three cars in the long driveway.

"James," the man called, "don't forget to call Miami from the office today. We have to have that new generator tomorrow at the latest."

"OK, Dad." He waved and drove off.

I was getting curious. The 'dads' sounded too genuine.

"You've been here for a while, I guess," I said.

"Yeah, I came to Negril twenty-five years ago. Man, there was nothing here but mosquitoes back then."

"So you came back every winter?"

"Hell, no," he seemed exasperated. "I live here, man. I've never once gone back to England. Why the hell should I?"

He seemed eager to talk. "Come on in, and I'll make you a cup of coffee, real Blue Mountain coffee. I know you tourists like that."

"What brought you here twenty-five years ago?" I asked, realizing that Negril, now a bustling town of several thousand, must have been little more than a swamp back then.

"Oh, I was an engineer with Kaiser Aluminum, based in Mandeville. A buddy and I would often go exploring the island. We came in here on mules."

"It must have been even more beautiful back then," I said.

"Yeah, wild; real virgin country."

He seemed to sense my mystification.

"I met my wife on that first trip here," he went on. "My buddy and I stayed with her parents, and she used to hang around me all the time. Shit, she was only fourteen or so, back then. I was old enough to be her father," he said, smiling at the memory.

"Not that old," I said, sizing him up to be forty-eight or so, at the most.

"Ha!" he laughed. "The climate's great here, but not that great. I'm sixty-two next week."

"You're joking," I said, not to flatter him. I was amazed. The man's skin was that of a young athlete—no flab whatever on his body.

A woman came into the kitchen.

"This is the wife," he said, and introductions were made.

I knew now why Mr. T. had never left town for twenty-five years. His wife was exceptionally striking. Having six children had done little damage to her figure.

"What do you do here?" I asked, realizing by now I was in the house of a successful man in the community.

"I build things," he said. "Well, these days I've been taking it a bit easy. I don't have as many projects as I used to have. But, see across the road?" He pointed to a foundation for a building. "I mess around with that. It's going to be a house for my oldest daughter. She's working in Kingston right now, but they have a baby on the way, and the wife wants her to live nearby. It's our way, you see," adding, "the Jamaican way, I mean."

"You think of yourself as Jamaican," I said.

"Well, of course," he said, slightly annoyed. "Look. I practically built Negril. Hell, I hate bragging, but I'm more of a Jamaican than most people who live here. I've been a citizen for twenty-three years, I built the first hotel here, Kaiser's, right on the beach and a dozen after that."

"You're a contractor?" I asked.

"Well, yes," he allowed, "but I also financed the bloody projects. I own them, you see."

It finally hit me that I was in the presence of the wealthiest man in Negril, maybe one of the wealthiest in the country.

"You can make money here," he said, "if you're not too lazy to work for it."

My eyes surveyed the property: the house was enveloped by a verandah; a dozen palm trees majestically dotted the estate. I marvelled at the ability of this white man to get things done in a land where it can take years to erect a simple house.

"Anybody with a brain in their head can do it," Mr. T. continued. "This is a wide open place, even now. Money talks. All this shit about lazy Jamaicans—sure they don't want to work if you don't pay them. They're too smart for that. The English exploited them for years. Pay them good dollars and they'll work their asses off. I always paid my men well, and then if they didn't work, I'd fire them and get somebody else."

It struck me that a key to his success was having a Jamaican wife. It gave him instant credibility. I glanced at the photo on the wall of a younger man and his sixteen-year-old bride. It was a scene right out of the romantic film, South Pacific.

"Have you ever yearned to go back to England?" I asked.

"Not really," he said, peeling a banana. "I guess what did it for me was my buddy, Charlie, going back to London after he retired from Kaiser, and writing me about how cold it was all the time. After a few months he got sick and, for Christ's sake, he died."

"I can't get over how you haven't changed much in the twenty-plus years since that picture was taken," I said. "Jamaica has been good to you."

"Well, I work hard, I eat nothing but fish and vegetables and fruit. I sleep like a log. I don't drink anything but a little scotch whiskey every night. This is paradise, my friend, the best climate in the world." Then, he laughed, adding, "Plus, a good woman keeps a man young."

He filled my coffee cup and I asked him, "Did you ever dream, when you came to Jamaica to work for Kaiser Aluminum, that you'd stay for the rest of your life?"

"Naw, I guess not. But I had no family left after the war. What the hell did I have to keep me back there?"

I thought of Mr. T. and his buddy, Charlie, deciding to go exploring by mule one day. And how that journey changed his life. If he had not been open to the new experience, would he now be retired in England, fighting arthritis or heart disease or cancer? Would he, like Charlie, not even be alive now?

Mr. T. had lucked out, yes. But he also had to muster the courage to go his own way and shun the lure of 'social services and pension' that England offered all of his contemporaries. He had to be willing to take a chance.

"I've been here for a couple of months now," I said, "and I really love this place. But to live here long-term? I don't know. I mean, you have to put up with so much bullshit—weeks for mail to arrive, haggles with everybody over prices, fending off every second person on the streets because you don't want to buy their drugs or trinkets, having to explain to everybody that you don't want a taxi, that you aren't staying at the Club Med, that you don't want to go on a rafting trip, and . . ."

"What do you expect, man?" he snapped, cutting me off. "People here are poor, they have to hustle. Sure, they see you as a mark, but after you've been here a while, they accept you and leave you alone. White men have no patience. That's the trouble."

I could see I offended him. And I realized that he was, indeed, accepted. His wife and kids and business interests attested to that. I still wondered whether an outsider, like myself, could ever find a home in Jamaica.

"What do you suggest I do to make a living here, then?" I asked. In spite of my ravings, I loved the country—the weather, the food, the ambience. It was a magical place.

"How much money do you have?" he asked with typical Jamaican candour.

"Oh, I suppose I could come up with twenty thousand." I decided to play the game.

"I can tell you how to make that a hundred thou' in a month."

I was all ears.

"You go to Miami," he said, "and you score twenty grand worth of cocaine . . ."

"Oh, come on," I interrupted, remembering the mess Hugh, who happened to live not far away, had made for himself.

He held up his hand. "I'm serious. You know nothing about how this country works." He spoke to me in a fatherly way now. "There's little risk. You see the Yanks aren't worried about what comes out of Miami, only what comes in. They tear apart planes coming in from here—all part of Reagan's drug crackdown."

"OK, but what about the Jamaican police?" I asked. I read every day about drug busts at the airport. While the society at large was disposed to drugs of all kinds, the official line was as hard as Reagan's.

Mr. T. laughed. "Hell, you give a Jamaican cop a twenty-dollar bill and he'll be blind as a bat. Give him a hundred and he'll carry your bags for you out of the airport."

He continued with his plan to make me rich and likely land me in jail to boot.

"When you get back to Negril, you unload the stuff and then sit back and watch your twenty grand become a hundred in no time flat."

"But who is going to pay that kind of money here?" I asked.

"Tourists," he shot back. "Americans, Germans, Canadians, anybody, staying at the ritzy hotels and looking for kicks. They don't want Jamaican ganja. Oh, sure, some do. But they want the hard stuff, and they're willing to pay."

"I think you're joking."

"Hell, no. You asked me a simple question. It's the surest way to make money I know of."

I couldn't tell whether he was serious or not. Part of me doubted he had earned his fortune by any illicit means; another part of me was not so sure.

We finished our coffee and I left to continue my run.

"You got any books?" he asked as I opened his gate.

"Books?"

"Yeah, it's real hard to find reading material here," he explained. "I've read all of Shakespeare in the last year. I'd like a change of pace from the classics. I've got more time on my hands now that I'm sort of retired."

"Sure, I'll drop off a few paperbacks next time as long as you promise to call off the little dogs."

John H. Davies—
A Man for All Seasons

Mr. T. was not the only example of eternal youth I encountered in my travels. John H. Davies was, in some respects, even more remarkable—and inspiring.

I have found Mexico to be full of surprises. It ranks as one of the world's best travel destinations. One reason for this is the hospitable, interesting people, both native Mexicans and transplants. John Davies was of the latter type.

One sunny winter day, I was sitting on a bench in the zocalo, or town square, of Taxco, once the silver capital of the world, and still a thriving town in a beautiful mountain setting. Some Zapotec dancers were performing their ancient rituals, their giant headdresses dominating the colourful costumes to the beat of a drum staccato.

An old man, white-haired and Mexican-looking, sat down beside me. We watched the dancers together for a while before he astounded me by saying in perfect English, "So you're the fellow from Ottawa."

"That's right," I said, taken aback, but realizing the old man probably got the information from some tourist I may have spoken to on an earlier visit to the zocalo, the meeting place for travellers in any Mexican town. Still the man's facility in English intrigued me.

"Well, sir," he went on, "I was born in Sandy Hill seventy-five years ago."

"Sure you were," I chided, "and I was born and raised in Mexico City."

I was certain he was putting me on, though Sandy Hill is, indeed, an older residential area in the centre of Ottawa, my hometown.

"You think I'm jesting, my friend," he countered, "but let me assure you I am as Canadian as you are. Hell, I went to McGill back in the days of Norman Bethune. I studied architecture."

I was still sceptical. This man looked as Mexican as Pancho Villa. We introduced ourselves.

"I've spent the past fifty years here," he told me.

I decided to let him play his little game.

As people passed by our bench, John had a word to say in Spanish to everybody. He was obviously well-known to locals.

"Fifty years, eh, John?" I tried not to smirk. Did this old fellow think I was born yesterday?

"Oh, yes. I love this town. I was even elected mayor for awhile many years ago," he said. "Look at it—wouldn't anybody in their right mind opt for a life in this gem of a place?"

I had to agree as I glanced at the majestic cathedral, the hilly cobblestone streets, the rolling hills and the azure sky. It was about twenty-four degrees celsius on this February day when the temperature in Ottawa was probably minus twenty-four. But I still felt this crafty old guy had learned all these details about Canada from someone else, probably the real John H. Davies.

I wondered how many other tourists he had tried this on. Did he have people from New York, Toronto and Medicine Hat in his repertoire too?

"Alright, John, let's hear the story of the Canadian from Sandy Hill, Ottawa, who went to McGill, knew Norman Bethune, became an architect, took a trip to Taxco fifty years ago and stayed."

John looked offended, frowned, but said, "Why don't we go to my apartment. We can talk over a drink, and you can look at my paintings if you like."

So he was trying to sell me paintings. No matter, I thought. At least he's entertaining. I had nothing else to do that morning.

"I'd like that very much," I answered.

I followed John up one of the steep streets. He pointed to a building on top of the hill. Starting to breathe heavily already, I wondered how my companion could possibly make it to the top. Ten minutes later, we were there, both panting and perspiring. I consoled myself that I might not be in inferior shape to this 75-year-old by telling myself he had adapted to the 6000-feet altitude over the years; I would also do so in time.

"When I first came to Taxco," John said, "there was hardly a road into the town, even though it had thriving silver mines nearby. When I laid eyes on this place, I fell in love with it. I knew instinctively I had found my niche."

"What about your architectural training?" I asked, my skepticism having more or less dissipated. "What about ties in Canada in Sandy Hill?"

"Ah, I always wanted to be an artist and a writer. I had a job with a firm in Montreal at the time, but I chucked it there and then."

"You mean to say you never went back?

"Oh, I went back a couple of times. I had a wife and a couple of kids. Responsibilities, eh? But I could never stay there after my first trip to Taxco. And so I just left."

"What about the family?"

"Oh, I wanted my wife to come here, too," he said, "but she was rooted in Canada. I had to leave."

We entered the apartment. It had the air of an artist's studio though hardly that of a seventy-five-year-old. The walls were lined with paintings, some hanging, but most propped against the walls. Many of the paintings were of an erotic nature: breasts and penises aplenty.

A large desk was strewn with paper. John was obviously a working artist/writer.

"I will make us drinks while you look at my paintings," he said, heading for the kitchen.

Look, I did. And I was dazzled. Many of the works featured men and women in sexual poses. Genitalia predominated. I guess it was John's age juxtaposed with the subject matter that initially surprised me. John's libido was certainly alive and well as the paintings seemed recently done.

"Well, what do you think?" he asked as he gave me my drink.

"I have to say I'm not an art connoisseur, but I find them stimulating."

That seemed to satisfy him. He nodded, "Good, that is art's first requirement—getting someone's attention. Now, is there one you particularly like?"

I chose one of the non-erotic ones—a scene of a young man on a mule, overlooking a town which looked like Taxco.

"Oh, that's one of my earlier works. I've had dozens of offers for that one. It's a self-portrait—that's me coming to Taxco!"

We sipped our drinks as I wandered about the apartment. I liked the functional set-up. Except for a few chairs, there was no furniture.

"When I'm not working or sleeping, I'm not here," John said. "I love the outdoor life in Mexico. I spend my time sitting in sidewalk cafés, wandering around the zocalo, walking in the hills." He added, impishly, "And occasionally being entertained in a senorita's flat!"

Had John H. Davies found the fountain of youth? I doubted I'd find his like in Sandy Hill today.

"When were you last in Canada?" I asked.

"It was when they were building Expo '67," he said. "My younger daughter had become an architect. Some of the buildings I designed back in the 'forties were still standing in Montreal. She asked me to work on a project with her. I agreed, mainly because I had seldom seen her as she was growing up."

"So you worked on Expo '67? That must have been interesting after so many years in Mexico."

"It was—especially getting to know my daughter," he allowed. "But, you know, I couldn't stand the winter. When the snow came, I found myself sitting at my drafting table thinking about this very room we're standing in and the scene we're looking at and one day I left my daughter's house for work and went to the airport instead."

We stood at the window overlooking the spectacular scene. John added, after a few moments, "My daughter was understanding. She even told me she had expected me to leave sooner.

"I have a son, too, you know," he went on. "He's a major in the Canadian Armed Forces. I haven't seen him in over ten years. He shares his mother's dislike of Mexico."

I realized I was talking to a man who had carved his own path. Some would, no doubt, describe him as selfish, even irresponsible. But he was happy and, indeed, healthy. He had changed the course of his life and accepted the consequences.

John moved across the room to his large desk, picked up a book, handed it to me and asked, "How's your Spanish?"

I admitted I possessed only a tourist's smattering of the language.

"Then I guess you can't read my book."

The book had a title in Spanish. I could make out *A History of Mexico*. The author's name was John H. Davies.

"When did you write this?"

"Oh, about thirty years ago," he said, "back when I travelled a lot in this country. I became so fascinated with Mexico that I wanted to see every corner of it. I spent a good five years on the road. Of course, I couldn't stay away from Taxco for more than a few months at a time.

"You had a real love affair with Mexico."

"Not had, my friend," he corrected me. "I am having a love affair with Mexico. It is not yet over."

I continued to look at the erotic paintings. John looked amused at my awkwardness in commenting about them.

"You Canadians are nervous when it comes to sex."

"I suppose you're right, John."

"That's part of my Canadian personality I managed to shake many years ago. Hell, I'm engaged to be married next month."

Surprised, I said, "Congratulations. Who is the lucky lady?"

"A pretty senorita from town," he said, a twinkle in his eye. He added, laughing, "I need a woman to keep me young, you see."

Our drinks finished, John saw me to the door. We had arranged to meet that evening for dinner in the zocalo.

As I was leaving, he asked, "Are you wondering how old my bride might be?"

"Yes, I'm curious."

"She's twenty-nine," he answered proudly.

Riding the Orient Express

Where does one catch the 'travel bug?' Sometimes summer trips with family will do it, or a holiday which surpasses all expectations.

It was a trip to Transylvania—Dracula country—that did it for me. It opened my eyes to what travel is all about: meeting interesting people, seeing exotic places and having unexpected things happen—every day.

Paris on Bastille Day, riding the fabled Orient Express from Paris to Budapest, meandering through the Romanian Alps in a beat-up Volkswagen, grappling with surly Hungarian border guards, exploring Black Sea beaches—wouldn't such a trip convert anyone to travel?

But I have to backtrack at this point—go back to seven years before I took The Plunge. I recall that I was reluctant to go on the six-week trip with two teaching colleagues. I had recently divorced and was busy establishing a different kind of relationship with my daughters. My plan to quit teaching had only recently been hatched, and so I was not in a position to spend a lot of money. I was doing some 'financial planning.' In short, it was a time of crisis and uncertainty in my life.

Two friends—Colin and Wayne—and I landed in Paris on Bastille Day, the French equivalent of the Fourth of July. Never had I seen such throngs in any street. There were bands galore, displays of military might, carousing, dancing. We had booked a hotel room for the day, thinking we should get some rest before our train journey. It turned out to be a waste of money. We could not have come up with a better antidote to jet lag. We joined in the party around ten in the morning and reluctantly made our way toward the Gare de l'est twelve hours later.

I had not yet learned one of the first rules of travel—travel light. Nor had my companions. Picture three grown men, more than slightly drunk from a day of 'Bastille-ing,' each carrying two large suitcases, bulling their way through the revellers.

We barely made it, actually stepping onto the Orient Express as it was pulling out!

The whole trip on the Orient Express—over twenty-four hours—was a feast in every way: good food, fascinating people, magnificent scenery, and countless unexpected happenings. What I remember most clearly was walking through the dozen or so cars that made up the famous train. From one to the other, you could savour a taste of France, or Germany, or even Turkey, depending upon where passengers were heading. Oddly, there were no Romanians or Hungarians on the train so far as I could see. But then, this was still the era of the Cold War.

This fact screamed out at us as the train stopped for an hour on the Austria/Hungary border while officious guards methodically went over each passenger's passport, eyeing them with a suspicion that seems absurd from today's vantage point. Soldiers used enormous mirrors to search under the train. For what, we weren't sure. The atmosphere was changing as the train moved eastward.

The food and drink were now not as plentiful, the train employees more surly. However, the border was a mere two hours from Budapest. And we all were excited, and a little apprehensive, about entering the Hungarian capital at midnight.

It presented such a contrast to the Paris scene we had witnessed the night before. Instead of crowded streets, we saw hardly a soul. Instead of bright lights, Budapest looked as if it was experiencing a power failure, almost a blackout. Even the railway station was subdued. A taxi driver silently drove us to the hotel where Wayne had reserved rooms. Again, driving through the dark streets was an eerie experience. Perhaps it was all geared to getting us in the mood for 'Dracula Country.'

Daylight produced a different Budapest. The view from our hotel, overlooking the Danube from the Buda side of the river, was breathtaking. Often referred to as the Paris of the East, Budapest is dominated by the beauty of the Danube in the same way as the Seine reigns supreme over Paris. The great river was a magnificent blue on that morning in July.

Food and music linger in my memory of Budapest: rich goulashes, free-flowing red wine, sumptuous desserts, and romantic violin music characterized the city's restaurants. It seemed that every second business establishment was an eating place. Wayne, always the historian, pointed out for us that since the revolution was squelched in 1958, most Budapest residents dwelt in very small flats, and thus ate out practically every night.

After a few dazzling days in Budapest, we left for Transylvania in a Volkswagen rental car on a rainy afternoon.

An hour out of the city, we noticed that the two front tires were completely bald. In our excitement, we'd neglected to check. It was pouring rain and beginning to get dark. We were still far from our intended destination, Cluj, capital city of Transylvania.

We noted the lack of traffic on the highway. As it got dark, the rain let up a little. I was driving, meeting the challenge of getting used to the car and the road.

In a short time, we reached the border and were to experience the first of many paranoia-induced hassles at borders in eastern Europe, the rule in the mid-seventies. Heavily-armed guards rifled through our bags, turned the car inside out, and spent a half-hour talking seriously among themselves about our travel documents. It was nerve-wracking—and a waste of time.

We finally got back on the road. After only a few kilometres, Colin yelled from the back, "Look, guys, up ahead."

"Gypsies! Wow!" Wayne exclaimed.

What we saw was a solitary horse-drawn wagon. What was so striking—and unnerving—was that there was no driver. At least we couldn't see one. The wagon was being pulled along on the shoulder of the highway. I slowed down as we passed it. There were no people to be seen. The horse just poked along as if going nowhere in no hurry.

"The gypsies travel at night," Wayne said, "to avoid being hassled, I suppose."

Evidently, gypsies did not rate as equal comrades in this Marxist-Leninist state. I had heard stories of wandering gypsies since childhood; now I was seeing the real thing.

As we drove, we passed, probably, a half-dozen similar driverless wagons.

We got to Cluj at one in the morning. It was a city of about a quarter of a million people and they were all in bed, it seemed. We managed to rouse a hotel keeper. He was irritable and suspicious. When he saw our Canadian passports, however, he agreed to give us a room, though he kept repeating that the hotel normally took no guests after ten o'clock. When I say "repeated," I am just assuming. We knew practically no Romanian.

When we got to our room, we realized he had given us the largest and most expensive room—call it a suite—in the hotel. The whole scene was right out of the nineteenth century: the decor, the furnishings, even the view from our window of the dimly lit city square.

We did not get the opportunity to sleep late. At six o'clock sharp, we were jolted awake by the sounds of hundreds of heavy boots marching on the cobblestone streets. I leaped out of bed, thinking war had broken out. From the balcony, I saw the army passing by, loudly singing a marching song. In a bygone day, royalty might have been standing right on my spot reviewing the troops. I was later to discover that marching soldiers were the rule at dawn in every Romanian town. No need to set an alarm clock.

We had yet another bizarre experience at breakfast. A man came up to our table, greeted us in broken English, and asked if he could join us.

"I sincerely hope you Canadian guests to our country are passing a pleasant time," he opened.

We assured him we were. He then proceeded to get right to the point; namely, what in the hell were we doing in Transylvania? He didn't believe we were here 'for pleasure.' Come to think of it, such a concept in Romania did seem farfetched.

"Gentlemen, permit me to inquire as to the type of employment you hold in Canada."

I resisted the temptation to tell the guy it was none of his business, deciding to go along. "We're all teachers," I responded.

He looked incredulous. "No, I mean what do you really do in your country?"

It seemed that since teachers in Romania were poorly paid, this interrogator, whose name was Vlad, felt we had to have another source of income.

"May I ask of you what price you paid for your airline tickets?"

Wayne answered this one. "I don't know what the equivalent would be in leis."

"Oh, I mean in dollars."

We hedged, asking the waitress for more toast.

Vlad was becoming a pain in the ass. A few questions later, he asked something that made the three of us instantly look at each other.

"You were fortunate to find gas for your Volkswagen at such a late hour last night."

Had this man been following us from the border and seen us gas up on the outskirts of Cluj, after looking for stations for the last hour of our journey? Or had our hotel room, as Wayne had suggested, been bugged?

I had a sudden, panic-ridden thought. I bolted from the table, headed for the lobby and ran up three flights of stairs, two steps at a time. While talking to our visitor, I had remembered leaving my passport and money in the room. If the room could be bugged, it could be opened.

I fumbled for the key, then opened the door. All of our stuff seemed there. I checked my wallet for my passport, other documents and money. I was astounded to see that it had been rifled through. I assumed I had been robbed but, after several checks, I realized nothing was missing. What had they been looking for? And who would simply leave cash behind?

Wayne and Colin had followed. They confirmed that their money belts had also been opened, but that nothing was missing.

When we returned to the table, Vlad was gone. Had he been the decoy? Was he a government official?

We later learned that roughly one person in three is a 'spy' of some sort, informing to somebody a little further up the ladder in a constant game of chalking up points with 'Big Brother.' Points that get you extra meat rations, travel opportunities, promotions, jobs for family members. Every visitor from the West is considered a spy. Why else would anyone be visiting Romania? No one would have believed the Dracula story, or the fact that the country was beautiful with mountains, valleys, quaint towns and ocean beaches.

Driving out of Cluj, we decided to keep our eyes peeled and wear our money belts at all times. We bandied about a number of responses to the "And what is your occupation?" question. Wayne was going to be a nuclear scientist, Colin, a military fighter pilot, and I, an aeronautical engineer.

As Colin drove, Wayne read excerpts from Bram Stoker's *Dracula*. The Irish writer had written his popular book about the infamous count in the nineteenth century without ever having visited Transylvania. He had researched the region painstakingly in the British Museum. He was, amazingly enough, directing us towards a town called Colabita, as Wayne read from the fabled book.

"There should be a crossroads up ahead," Wayne said. Sure enough, there was. "Take the left fork," he directed.

The road turned to dirt and was pot-holed beyond belief. Our car was doing the job though. And the scenery was spectacular, Swiss-like in its mountain ambience. Farms dotted the hillsides. Occasionally, we'd pass a shepherd with his flock of sheep beside the road. They were dressed much as they probably had been a hundred years before. Time seemed to be standing still.

After meandering through the hills all afternoon, we pulled up at what appeared to be the barracks of a Collective Farm which bore the name, Colabita. The decor of the buildings belied the natural beauty of the surroundings. There seemed to be several grey, quonset-like structures made out of cement blocks. One had a sign and was bedecked with the Romanian flag which, with its hammer and sickle, was more or less a copy of that of Romania's giant neighbour, the USSR.

We guessed it might be the administrative centre and so entered, wondering if we'd be able to find some beds for the night and, ideally, some dinner.

We needn't have worried. It seemed we were expected. News travels faster than one would think in Transylvania. An official in the building told us in passable English that we were at that moment in Communist Party Headquarters, that we should surrender our passports so that the required documentation could be done and that we would be taking our meals at the central workers dining hall. He would show us where we'd sleep.

He was neither friendly nor hostile. His manner reminded me of a civil servant processing some bureaucratic document: Let's get this damned thing out of the way.

The room for the night turned out to be right upstairs. It was furnished with three single beds, complete with linen, and a solitary lightbulb. We decided to head for the dining hall.

Resembling a huge cafeteria, the hall was packed with families who, presumably, had just returned from a day in the fields. A radio blared out a program that sounded like the six o'clock news.

People stared at us curiously. We nodded and smiled. Some returned our smiles.

The meal consisted of some tasteless gruel, looking a little like pork and beans that had been left out in the pouring rain. It tasted as good as it looked.

We managed to finish and were suddenly joined by a woman who addressed us in French. We exchanged greetings. She was a sort of public relations person, she explained. She had served abroad in the Romanian embassy in Brussels where she had learned her French. Indeed, she outshone the three of us in her fluency.

"And so, gentlemen, why have you come to this place?" she asked, after a few pleasantries.

Here we go again, I thought. "We are tourists," I answered, "and have wanted to come to Transylvania for many years."

"Of course, Romania has many tourists," she said, smiling ironically, "but never has anyone come to Colabita," adding, "as there is nothing here worth seeing."

Wayne spoke up. "Have you heard of Bram Stoker, the novelist who wrote about Dracula?"

She looked at us as if to say, "Stop putting me on."

"Yes," Colin went on, enthusiastically, "we actually followed the directions in his book to this very place."

"So this famous writer is Romanian?" she asked.

"Oh, no," Wayne said, "he was Irish. He never even visited Transylvania. He wrote the book in England."

"And gave you directions," she finished Wayne's sentence for him, with a bit too much sarcasm for our liking.

"Yes, and precise directions they were, even though they were written over sixty years ago," I added.

Her face got red.

"I fear I must report you to the District Manager," she said. "My time is too valuable to have such joking."

We looked at one another, unsure of how to establish our credibility with this humourless, officious woman. It was taking us some time to catch on: people did not travel to Transylvania just for pleasure, or even for 'literary' reasons.

"We are teachers," I tried again. "We teach the geography of Europe. Transylvania has always been an important region in our courses."

Wayne's mouth had dropped. He was suppressing a grin.

"In that case," the woman said, "why was the Ministry of Education not informed? None of your documents indicate the educational nature of your journey."

"Maybe that's the one that disappeared when we were robbed in Cluj," Colin chipped in.

"Robbed! You must be joking," said the woman, whose face was now even redder.

We explained what had occurred in the hotel earlier.

"Then where is the police report of the robbery?"

This was becoming aggravating. Paranoia was personified in this woman.

We succeeded in escaping to our room, leaving our gestapo-like interrogator at the table, a bewildered look on her face.

"Next thing it'll be the police waking us in the middle of the night," Wayne said.

No one woke us up that night, though the mosquitoes tried hard, entering our screenless window at will. As if we needed any more 'atmosphere,' we had gone to sleep with Wayne reading aloud excerpts from Dracula. If only that room had been bugged, we'd have been off the hook!

For the next few weeks, as we explored many back roads of Romania, not a single day went by that wasn't filled with all the ingredients of travel at its best —the people, the places and, most of all, the unexpected. And to think I had almost passed it up!

Days at the Office

The years after I quit my college teaching job were not all filled with trips to exotic places. At regular intervals, the bank account had to be replenished. I still harboured the idea that I might find some full-time, stimulating job that I could enthusiastically throw myself into.

Recently, I found myself in a nine-to-five office job. I had never worked in an office before but, after a teaching stint in Africa (more about that later), circumstances landed me—not just in any office job—in a government office job! After all my past civil service bashing!

Still, I was happy to have the work at the time. I needed the money and was at loose ends since returning from Africa.

But I found the experience quite distasteful, though there were some amusing aspects to the job. I didn't take to the bland blue/grey/white decor. Nor the air conditioning (it made my eyes itch). Nor the hours (being cooped up inside for the best eight hours of the day!). Nor the constant sitting (never had my rear end been so sore). Nor the putting in time filling the hours (I had very little to do, even though I was told we were understaffed!). Nor, finally, the work itself—it was unspeakably dull. Although I had been hired as a 'writer,' I was convinced after one day that a good grade twelve student could do the job.

The money was very good, the people I worked with were friendly and there was no pressure (other than the fear of falling asleep). So I was determined to make the best of it.

It was the 'doing nothing' that really grated on me. After a month, I had still failed to adjust and become one of the 'happy workers' my colleagues seemed to be. Was I a slave to the work ethic? Why couldn't I, like my office mates, learn how to kill time between assignments. Mind you, I did have about an hour-and-a-half of work to do every day. Still, that left about six hours to put in before heading home.

In the first couple of weeks, I had read three weighty novels, written several long-overdue personal letters, composed a few articles for possible publication, taken several two-hour lunches, tried ridiculously-extended coffee breaks, read several newspapers every day (the section I worked in was Communications, and so stocked all the major newspapers), attempted to socialize with fellow paper pushers and talked on the telephone more than usual. I was running out of diversions.

Maybe I'm just a creature of habit. Jobs I had worked at in the past hadn't been so slack. As a teacher, I could never get to the bottom of the pile of student essays on my desk. I could never find enough time to properly plan a lesson. To talk to students. To even go to the bank. As a waiter, I recall practically collapsing after a busy day during my two-month stint. As a carpenter's helper, toiling under the hot sun, I remembering savouring the fifteen-minute breaks allotted morning and afternoon. As a newspaper reporter, I practically sweated blood as deadlines approached.

It was good not to be run off my feet, but this was ridiculous! On my first day at the office, I had been warned by a co-worker: "Geez, what a time for you to start. Ralph is going on holidays next week. You'll be on your own." I had spent all my first week dreading the work-load I would be compelled to carry when the other writer in the office was away.

I can report that I managed quite well. In fact, I perceived no increase at all in my work-load. Was every job in the government double-staffed, I wondered? What would life there be like when Ralph returned? What would I say when he asked me how I got along carrying the whole load on my shoulders? "It was rough, Ralph. Good to have you back, big guy!"

So why didn't I simply ask for more work? Well, I did. And I was admonished to "enjoy the break," and warned "you'll be too busy to breathe most of the time here." Oh, well . . .

And so with a dearth of work to do, I set out to create fruitful ways of filling the time. In addition to the activities mentioned already, I discovered that diversions sought me out if I simply sat at my desk staring at my computer. For instance, the new boss dropped by one day. Since I had already been on the job three weeks when she arrived, I felt obliged to welcome her to our little section. It's called Creative Services.

Here is what Sylvia said, with only a few nods from me interrupting her flow:

"I'm really excited about being chosen to manage this unit. I know that understaffing is one of your main worries, and so rest assured, I'm going to get some more bodies in here. You guys must be going nuts. There's really nobody steering the ship right now. You know, I have a wealth of experience in this field, but I've decided to, realistically, give myself a few weeks to get up to speed. I'm throwing myself into this job. When I was in here on Sunday—by the way, it's incredible how much work you can get done when nobody's around—it dawned on me that the furniture in my office is, well, it just isn't me. It has to go. I guess you've already noticed that if there's one thing that characterizes me as a manager, it's that I am a real stickler for detail. But, you know, it works. It really does. I just know things will pick up when I get more bodies for us."

I could go on. Sylvia probably didn't notice the look of incredulity on my face as I tried to decide whether she was putting me on or not. Could she actually be serious? Before she left, I promised her I'd do my best to keep the ship floating until she got us more bodies. I managed to resist saying, "I think I should soon be up to speed."

I decided I should avoid Sylvia as much as possible.

There was a large shopping mall right under the office—well, sixteen floors down, on the bottom floor of the gigantic tower. I was free to explore it on prolonged coffee breaks. In trying to find the post office in the mall one day, I noted the variety of shops in the labyrinth down there. And the hoards of people. Window shopping and people watching—just the thing for the bored office worker, except the artificial atmosphere there exceeded that of the offices above!

Often I went outside on my breaks, and always during lunch hour. I learned to appreciate the sights, sounds and smells of the real environment after being locked up in that depressing office. Real trees. Real wind. Heat. Rain. I'd listen to birds chirping. I'd watch men actually working on a construction project nearby. I revelled in the tangy aroma of sizzling hot dogs which emanated from an outdoor vendor's grill.

I soon ran out of ways to kill time, though. But I was not yet ready to toss in the towel and relinquish the pleasure of the bi-weekly pay cheque.

Ralph had returned and, as I suspected, my work-load did not change at all. I still found myself with an average of six hours to kill every single day. Thirty a week. I saw it as a challenge. Was I up to it? Should I even try to meet it? Should I simply walk out the door, wave goodbye to Sylvia and say, "Sorry, I have better ways to spend my time."

Surely there had to be some valid reason to justify doing this dreary, meaningless work.

I had no mortgage. Elaine and I had developed a simple lifestyle. We could live on less than half what I was earning. And time was passing. Yes, there was the rub. I had observed my fiftieth birthday that year. I craved for something to throw myself into.

This job was never going to be the answer. I came up with a 'survival technique' one day. I decided to regard the job as a temporary 'building up the war chest' endeavour. Make money for three months and then travel. Escape the brutal Canadian winter. It might work—but only if I could avoid going crazy in the time remaining at the office.

In the meantime, I decided to use my spare hours there in front of my computer to recount recent experiences which were more than just putting in time.

What should I write about? I pondered. My mind headed immediately to memories of that recent year Elaine and I spent in Africa. Our time there had been fascinating and I hadn't had the opportunity to make an appropriate record. This could turn out to be more than a diversion. I could be 'creative' right there in my office at Creative Services!

Chindunduma

Elaine and I went to Zimbabwe some seven years after I took The Plunge. An opportunity with a Canadian NGO, or non-governmental organization, presented itself. We were both excited about exploring Africa, even if it meant I'd have to teach again and Elaine would find herself back in nursing.

When I thought of Africa, sitting in the office in front of my computer a year or so after returning to Canada, I remembered vividly my initiation to that fascinating continent: a bumpy ride in the back of a large flatbed truck—called a lorry there—in the pitch-dark night from Harare, the capital, to the rural school where I was assigned to teach English, three hours away in the bush. The fires burning by the roadside were spectacular (it was the dry season), and the smells and sounds emanating from the villages near the road were exotic. We had only a few hours before stepped off a plane from Canada.

Chindunduma is the name of a school in northeast Zimbabwe where Elaine and I were headed, along with about a dozen Zimbabweans, huddled together in the back of the lorry. I assumed they, too, had something to do with the school. I had been introduced to one or two of them. They were polite and welcoming, but seemed to be silently asking, "What in the world are you people doing here?"

Chindunduma—the name means Ever Angry in the native tongue, Shona—is a boarding school for about seven hundred students and had been established during the struggle for independence, in the late 1970s, to allow guerilla fighters to receive an education. I had been sent there not just because there was a shortage of qualified teachers in the country, but also because the place was so remote that even native Zimbabwean teachers tried to avoid being assigned there.

The nearest town was sixty kilometres away, partly over a dirt road. There were thirty-five teachers at the school, including six or seven other expatriates from Britain, Ireland, Germany and Holland. The only transportation was the school truck we were riding on, and two cars belonging to German teachers.

We would soon learn that the main topic of conversation at the school was transportation. When is the truck going to town? Or, who has reserved space with the Germans for the grocery shopping trip on Saturday?

Even before arriving at the school, I wondered why these African kids were being educated to pass the British Cambridge exams. Why had they adopted the system of their colonial oppressors? Wasn't there good African literature? I had many questions on my mind, and no small measure of apprehension as I adjusted a suitcase under my bottom while the truck bounced along the road.

We had come to Africa for the adventure, having yearned for years to travel there. What better way to experience a new place than to live and work there? You're guaranteed to get close to the people and to meet them in a way no tourist could. This posting was perfect for us.

As the truck rolled on in the night, I felt an elation I had rarely felt before. The bags of corn meal, or maize, provided a backrest. Cold bottles of the local beer were passed around, everybody taking a swig and passing the bottle on. A sense of camaraderie ensued. The fires continued to burn all around us. Apparently, most were intentionally started in the belief that a burnoff before the rains came would be good for the soil. Maybe so, but they were dangerous. One of my fellow passengers told me that every year whole villages were wiped out by out-of-control brush fires.

There seemed to be lights from buildings up ahead: it had to be the school. The truck came to a stop with people jumping off in every direction. It was too dark to discern houses, people's faces or the general landscape. Someone grabbed our luggage. It was all a bit eerie. We were led to a house which had a single light and not one piece of furniture. No problem, we were told, somebody was going to fetch school mattresses for us and a couple of desks would serve as a table to eat off. We had brought a two-burner stove, or hot plate, with us and a few utensils. Someone else arrived with a mosquito net and adeptly hung it from the ceiling, over our mattresses on the floor.

It was late. A neighbour came by to invite us to her house for dinner. Another man, whose face I couldn't see clearly in the dark, shook our hands, saying, "Welcome to this place, comrades." Comrades, I noted. So—what the hell—I answered, "Thanks, comrade. Good to be here."

We were touched by the kindness and warmth of our hosts. After all, we were white and we looked like the very oppressors the Zimbabweans had only recently struggled to defeat. Ever Angry—well, perhaps the anger had dissipated in the joy of victory and the thrill of being in charge of their own country at long last.

I fell asleep trying to picture what Chindunduma would look like in the light of day.

Suffice to say, I could never have imagined it. I leaped out from under the mosquito net as I awoke to bright rays of sunshine flooding the room. Running to the window, I was stunned by the dazzling plethora of bright red bougainvillaea outside the window, practically growing into the house. Beyond was a giant tree with purple flowers! I was to learn later that the tree was a jacaranda. It contrasted stunningly with the bougainvillaea.

I saw several buildings, all made of cement blocks of an ugly grey colour, and beyond, beautiful rolling hills burnt brown by the heat and sun. The drab collections of buildings, no doubt classrooms and dormitories, didn't seem to fit into the natural beauty of the surroundings.

I opened the door and stepped out onto a porch. A woman walked by with a container of water on top of her head. She smiled and said, "Mangwanani"—good morning. Somehow I knew we were going to like this place.

And like it we did. But not right away. For the first while, the isolation took some getting used to. Weeks went by. Except for trips to town to buy supplies, life consisted of teaching classes all day, grading students' work, meal preparations, a daily walk through the bush at four in the afternoon when the heat subsided enough to allow it and, above all, the constant socializing. Fellow teachers and school support staff would all drop in unannounced. As would even villagers from close by, people who lived in mud huts with thatched roofs and were exceedingly curious about foreigners from exotic, far-away lands, like America, which they insisted on calling Canada.

Our Western notions of privacy went out the window in the closed quarters of the school community. Elaine and I discovered that the only time we were ever alone was when we slipped under the net at night. Meals were always interrupted. Neighbouring children would saunter in and help themselves to a fruit from a bowl on the table.

Stepping outside always meant a conversation, solicited or not. An invitation to drop over for a beer. A discussion about who was going into town tomorrow. A student requesting assistance. A groundskeeper asking if he could borrow your cassette player. It was an unnerving experience for us so conditioned to privacy, so used to a caller announcing his or her arrival by telephone. We felt like goldfish in a glass bowl, but gradually our world became Chindunduma.

We came to enjoy the camaraderie of the school in the African bush. Whites and blacks blended in a way inconceivable in a less-isolated environment. Perhaps it was that we really needed each other. Maybe it was that there was nothing to be possessive, or suspicious, about. Lodging was the same for all. Practically nobody owned a car. Except for the headmaster, nobody was the boss. There was nothing to aspire to and nothing to fear. Nothing to hide. Everybody depended on the school lorry for transportation, drank the local beer, played darts, tended a small garden, taught the same kids (or fed them, or cleaned their quarters).

Perhaps because of the lack of outside stimuli, the people at the school tended to be rather candid. And so, we came to experience a type of communal life that has virtually disappeared. In talks on the porch in the cool of the night, a young Zimbabwean colleague might drop by to lament about problems in his love life (everybody knew he was enamoured of the school secretary); or another teacher might speak in detail of the horrors her village underwent in the ten-year war, or liberation struggle. She had gone off to fetch water one afternoon, as a teenager, and returned to find the village in flames and her parents dead.

In turn, we would talk about our homesickness for family and friends far away in Canada. Or try to explain such terms as 'junk food,' or 'couch potato.' ("I do not understand how any food can be regarded as junk!" a fellow teacher would insist.) Or answer countless questions about life in our country, explaining that having plenty of everything did not necessarily make people happy. (They didn't believe us!)

Our neighbour, a math teacher, would quietly tell us about his leaving home, at age fifteen, to join the 'freedom fighters,' as we, so privileged to have grown up in safe, stable Canada, listened in awe.

Several of the 'expats' had equally interesting stories to tell. A young Englishman, Nick, had decided one day, while on the way to his London job as a waiter in a ritzy restaurant, to volunteer to come to Africa and teach—even though he had no teaching credentials or experience. His warmth and sense of humour were a source of pleasure to all at Chindunduma. He regaled us with stories of his off-beat upbringing. His mother had taken him and his sister on a 'pilgrimage' to Memphis, Tennessee, to visit Graceland, home of Elvis, when Nick was in his teens. He'd stayed in Memphis and gotten a job as a DJ at a local radio station. Music was his passion and his enormous collection of tapes provided background music during the long evenings spent socializing on the porch.

As the mosquitoes buzzed around us, night after night, we came to appreciate the pleasures to be derived from conversation, something, we realized, we'd let slide somewhat in our lives in Canada. Here there was simply nothing else to do: no televisions, telephones, shopping centres, automobiles. Not even strong enough lighting to read by.

Chindunduma gave a new dimension to the term, 'changing your reality-matrix.' If only my old boss, Doreen, could see me now!

Shall We Dance?

A party was held to welcome new staff early in the term and our hosts pulled out all the stops.

All day long on the Saturday of the party, there was an air of anticipation. Women scurried about, co-ordinating the food preparations. The men frantically organized the purchasing of the booze, arguing about how much to buy, what kinds, how to keep the beer cold and how to keep the drinkers from starting too soon. Others busied themselves collecting and making tapes for the music of the evening, rigging up loudspeakers, arranging tables and chairs—all outdoors, of course. No need to worry about rain here. It was the middle of the dry season.

As the afternoon wore on, the excitement pitched. It was as if the president were coming for a visit. Our neighbour invited me for a beer. "Just to get in the mood, brother." Women followed one another to the outdoor showers to do their hair. Some of the men frantically cut wood for cooking the meat and the national dish, sadza, a maize-based porridge-like staple. The DJ was checking his sound system. All this and it was only four o'clock! Four more hours until party time.

The party did start on time, perhaps the only thing in Africa that always does. By eight, many of the Zimbabwean males were already well on the way to an early intoxication while the women were busy sampling the finger foods laid out on the tables. The men talked and laughed noisily, either standing around or dancing to the blaring music. The women whispered and giggled shyly, seated in chairs when they weren't eating the goodies. There was little intermingling of the sexes.

Darkness comes to southern Africa early. And so the lighting for the party was perfect. The moon shone brightly in a sky flooded with stars. One or two dim spotlights illuminated the dancing area. The sounds of Oliver Mutukudzi and Thomas Mapfumo rang out in the night. The eight or nine of us 'expats' seemed content to fade into the background, watching the local men dance together. Not a single woman took to the dance floor.

Gradually, a few white couples danced. Somehow this seemed to emphasize our 'apartness.' I was standing to the side sipping my beer when I found myself part of a group of male dancers, one of whom was the slightly drunk headmaster. Our eyes met. He smiled and seemed to invite me to join the little circle. It all reminded me of the way one might circle the ice in a pick-up hockey game back home, eyeing the person with the puck, waiting for a pass or an invitation to join in. The music throbbed. Was the headmaster trying to see how 'cool' this Canadian teacher was? So far, he had ignored me at Chindunduma. I had attributed this to a combination of shyness, a desire to appear 'chief-like,' and perhaps fear that I might be one of the all-too-common do-gooders—the type overflowing with messianic zeal and dedicated to teaching these 'poor Africans' how to run their schools.

I found myself swaying to the music. The headmaster did not take his eyes off me. My eyes remained glued to his. I felt nicely loose, relaxed. I recalled hearing that Mr. Ngitimana had been a guerilla fighter during the war, and had been a founding father of the school over ten years ago. He had been a marksman who routinely carried out solitary missions for the purpose of blowing up Rhodesian military installations. He had a ferocious face, marred by a couple of ugly scars. Yet his eyes were kind, if somewhat fierce and penetrating.

I let myself imitate his every movement to the beat of the music. He was leading, I was following. He was teaching, I was learning. He began to smile as he saw that I was, if not a great dancer, at least, a game one. I felt completely unselfconscious, free. Sweat poured off my face as I raised my bottle to my lips for much-needed sustenance.

In a matter of moments, I found myself dancing, more or less, with the headmaster, from a distance now of only a few feet. When the music stopped, he approached me and suddenly put a bear hug on me, practically knocking my beer loose from my hand.

"It is good that you are here, comrade. Thank you for coming to help us."

I tried to return his greeting, but was somewhat speechless, the wind having been almost knocked out of me.

"Thank you for having us here," I managed to say. "This is a great party!"

I was so conditioned by my Canadian experience of seeing school adminis-trators as pompous, stuffed shirts that I hardly knew how to respond to his raucous warmth. Several bystanders laughed approvingly. I seemed to have passed some sort of test.

By this time, the dance area was overflowing, but the Zimbabwean women were nowhere to be seen. I shouldn't have been surprised. It hadn't taken long to see the abysmal status of African women. The men ruled the roost, and the term feminism had not yet entered into the African lexicon. Even in school, the male students dominated to the point that girls were afraid to answer questions in class.

As the night wore on, I came to feel more and more at home. I joined a group of men. They were comparing drinking exploits. Allowing for beer-induced exaggeration, the figures being bandied about were awe-inspiring or disgusting, depending on your point of view. "Yes, man, it is true," exclaimed the chemistry teacher, "I have been with him. Gibson did, indeed, drink nineteen Castles in an evening!" Another responded, "No, that is a lie. I have drunk with Gibson and I am certain that if he drank over a dozen, he would be flat out." Uproarious laughter, followed by yet another tale of somebody else's drinking prowess. I had consumed about a half-dozen bottles of Castle—the good, local beer—and was feeling no pain.

Around midnight, the food was served, an event in itself. A cow had been slaughtered for the occasion, as well as a pig. Meat, or nyama, as it is called in Zimbabwe, is a symbol of prosperity. And people devoured the mounds of it laid out on huge platters! Accompanying items, such as vegetables and bread and fruit, were left until last. Plates were loaded and the dance area was soon deserted.

When the music resumed, I noticed that some of the Zimbabwean women began to dance in little circles of four or five. The men were now sitting, immobilized by their food and drink, talking quietly now or dozing. It was as if the women had been given a signal to dance, perhaps as a reward for preparing the feast.

I was about to call it a night when I spotted the woman whom I had seen carrying water on her head on our first morning at the school. She was stunning in her native dress, her hair piled high on her head in a sort of bun. She was swaying to the music, her eyes partly closed. I found myself staring, moving to the beat, too. Our eyes met, but she immediately averted hers. Would it be proper for me to ask her to dance? Would it be a friendly gesture on my part? Or an insult? A few of the black males had danced with white women. Didn't it work both ways? I considered asking a British colleague, but did not. I was so new here. Would he think me an idiot? He'd either say that it isn't done. Or he'd exclaim, "Why not, mate?" I realized I had a lot to learn at Chindunduma.

It seemed that the men paid little attention to their women in public. If I had asked the beautiful water carrier to dance, she would probably have looked at the ground, and then giggled. She would have assumed I was making a joke. The thought made me feel a tinge of sadness on an otherwise joyful evening.

I decided to go home to bed at about three o'clock in the morning, only slightly miffed that Ngitimana did not ask me for the last dance.

A Night at Mavis' House

Because of the school's remote location, life seemed to revolve around what we came to refer to as the "T. Word"—Transportation. It was no problem if you were one of the two teachers who owned a car, but with no public bus service for miles around, practically all of us were dependent on the school lorry and the whims of its driver, the headmaster and the truck itself, with its assorted mechanical idiosyncrasies.

Transportation was the subject of tea-break conversations, late-night chatting on the porch, brief exchanges while walking to class and across-the-yard-while-watering-your-garden talks. The subject always came up for discussion in staff meetings. Or when you met one of the car owners on the path. It was all-consuming.

And it was important. As much as we had adjusted to the rigours of life in the bush, we were still subject to our conditioned reliance on basic amenities: staple food items, toothpaste, toilet paper and beer. You can survive on powdered milk and week-old bread. You can adjust to the absence of newspapers or peanut butter. But there is a bottom line. And it always came into play as the two-week supply of provisions ran low.

It wasn't so much the need to have a ride out of Chindunduma—you could walk six kilometres of dirt road to the tarmac and probably hitch a ride on a passing truck, if you were not in a great hurry. You could usually get to Bindura, the nearest town with a market. The problem was getting back home, laden with groceries. Not only was the food supply heavy, several items were eminently perishable in the intense heat of the day. And then, we had heard stories of stranded teachers having to spend the night sleeping on the floor of a bottle store—the Zimbabwean term for beer store—about thirty kilometres away. Not something we aspired to.

And so, one Friday afternoon as Elaine and I left the school on a weekend trip to Harare, we were feeling almost euphoric. We had been assured of a ride from the bottle store on Sunday night by none other than the headmaster himself. "Don't worry, comrade, there will be transportation from Madziwa on Sunday evening at six," he promised. We could rest easy.

Not that our Harare trip was strictly rest and recreation. We had not been to the capital in over a month. We wanted to buy a second-hand fridge and arrange for it to be picked up by the school lorry. We had to find accommodation in Harare, do our grocery shopping, pick up books which had finally arrived from Canada, try to make phone calls to our families back home, straighten out a salary mix-up at the Department of Education offices, and attempt to get a parcel from Ottawa out of Zimbabwe Customs, as it had been tied up for a month in red tape.

But we were riding a high! We had transportation back to Chindunduma arranged.

And we had a wonderful weekend. Everything fell into place. We had savoured a touch of civilization: a movie, some restaurant dinners, a swim in a posh hotel's pool, strolls in the evening without fear of stepping on poisonous snakes and reassuring phone conversations with family in Canada. We even managed to buy a coveted second-hand fridge, which the school lorry would pick up on its next trip to town. We were in fine spirits, ready to return to Chindunduma on Sunday afternoon.

A three-hour bumpy bus ride got us to Madziwa—home of Victor's bottle store—our provisions stashed, precariously, on the roof. We tried not to think of the blazing sun melting our frozen meat and fish. By four o'clock, we were guzzling our first cold beer at Victor's. We had made it with two hours to spare!

Victor had allowed us to put our supplies in a corner of his freezer. Everything was jelling. Five o'clock found us well into our third Castle and enjoying the scene while sitting outside on beer crates in the shade of a huge mango tree chatting it up with locals, waiting for Ngitimana's transportation to arrive around six.

One of the German teachers arrived. Ironically, she had space in her car. We naturally declined her offer of a ride.

"No thanks," Elaine said, "the lorry is coming in an hour or so."

And so we waited. Six o'clock came. No truck. No matter. Time is different here—African time.

Seven o'clock came. We started to squirm, just slightly, fighting that sinking feeling in the pit of our stomachs. It got dark. Maybe he'd been detained by a problem at the school. He'd show up. We nibbled on some snacks. But Chindunduma seemed somehow farther away than its thirty kilometres from Madziwa.

I was now regretting passing up the German's offer two hours ago. Still, Ngitimana would hardly leave us stranded, abandoned to sleep on Victor's floor. It wasn't even as if we had solicited the offer of transportation. It had come from him with no prompting. From his heart, so to speak.

Victor's was clearing out. As is the custom, most patrons left only when their money had run out or when they were 'zonked'—the local term for badly drunk.

We weren't zonked. But we were worried. And angry. We were fuming, vowing that we'd transfer out of the isolated hell hole that Chindunduma had —in our frustrated minds—become in the past two hours. Weren't we here to help? Weren't we giving up the comforts of our Canadian lives for this? Didn't we deserve at least honesty? Why had he promised to pick us up? We were starving, tired and head-achy from too much beer.

It was now nine o'clock. Worried, I broached the subject of accommodation with Victor as he wearily counted the day's receipts. "Do not be worried, my friend," he said. "You are our guests and we will look after you!"

Sure, I thought, as my eyes scanned the filthy floor, and the mosquitoes buzzed in seeming anticipation of a night's feast. Victor shoved a cold beer in each of our hands. We thanked him, weakly.

The hospitality of these people touched us even in our frustration. In our four hours there, countless people had approached us to talk, offer to buy us beer and share food with us. Now the bar owner was cautioning us not to worry.

As we were sitting dejectedly, conjuring up ways of getting even with the headmaster, a woman sidled up to us, plunking herself down beside us. She was stinking drunk.

Sticking her hand in my face, she slobbered, "Hello, man, I be Mavis. Who be this lady?"

Assured she was my wife, she smiled, shrugged and said, "No matter. Mavis going to take care of both of you tonight."

We introduced ourselves with some hesitation, doubting Mavis could take care of herself tonight.

"You and your missus stay at my house tonight."

We both stared at her, our bottles suspended in mid-air.

"Yes, people," she slurred, "Victor ask me to give you place to sleep. I say, sure, as long as you buy me a beer."

Well, one beer turned out to mean three. It was well past eleven when we found ourselves trying to follow Mavis' weaving path through the night to her house.

"How far is your place, Mavis?"

"Oh, not far, my friends," she giggled. "Just follow me."

Not an easy task when you can't see your hand in front of you. The groceries weighed a ton. We were exhausted. And just who was Mavis? Should we be following her off into the bush? We were beyond caring. I just wanted a place to sleep for the night before we got a lift to the school where I was going to perform a most unprofessional act: I was going to kill the headmaster. Or something like that.

Mavis talked incessantly. "So you be Canadian. Ha! I know a Canadian. His name be Roy Garfield," she yelled into the still night. "I loved Roy Garfield. Yes, I did. But he a liar. He tell me he come back for me, a whole year ago, when he move to Botswana. That bastard. He no good. Man, I loved that guy."

After a fifteen-minute walk, we arrived at what seemed to be a house. It was hard to tell. Only a faint light came from what must have been the living room.

Mavis hollered at someone in a bedroom nearby. A man emerged whom Mavis introduced as her uncle, Rodney. He must have been ten years younger than she. Oh, well, I still took everything at face value in Africa. I just wanted to sleep.

"You two sleep here," Mavis said, as she led us into a musty, hot room. "I take the couch." And she stumbled off, yelling, "Many teachers stay at Mavis' place." Again she laughed throatily.

We were beginning to catch on. Our hostess did not exactly rent rooms. It might be an interesting night, we thought, as we tried to adjust the cardboard in one window to keep out the mosquitoes.

"Mavis," Elaine had protested, "we can't take your bed."

"Don't worry, missus," she answered. "Mavis have no trouble going to sleep tonight. You people be comfortable."

We thanked her and said good night.

Then the fun began.

Though we fell asleep almost at once, we were awakened shortly by a tap on the cardboard over the window.

"Mavis, Mavis, honey," someone whispered, "I be here, baby."

Imagine the guy's response when I whispered back, "Use the front door. Mavis is in the living room."

I could picture the man's look of shock. He replied, "Sorry, brother, sorry," adding, "I come back later, Mavis."

All night long, variations of this theme occurred. Mavis was taking care of more people than us tonight. She was a popular woman in Madziwa.

In the morning, we offered Mavis some money as we packed up our now-dripping groceries. Not only had we accepted her hospitality, but we had acted as a deterrent to her regular flow of business. Now sober, she was no less gracious and generous than she had been last night. She steadfastly refused even a few dollars.

"We here to help each other, people," she insisted. "I tell you what I like. I like to come to Chindunduma sometime and visit at your house. I like that so much."

We left with the understanding that Mavis would come up to the school one day. As for our transportation fiasco, it hadn't been such a catastrophe after all. It could have been worse. As we rode in the back of a school supply truck we hitched a ride with after walking back to Victor's, we agreed we'd had an experience to remember. Still, I promised myself I'd exact my pound of flesh from Ngitimana as soon as we got back to Chindunduma.

The problem was, the matter never came up! Taking Ngitimana to task about our transportation problem just didn't seem like the thing to do when I met him in the hall later that day and was greeted by his smiling, "I trust you and your wife had a pleasant weekend in Harare."

What could I say?

On the Job in Zimbabwe

Not high on my list of reasons for going to Zimbabwe was teaching itself, as I had left teaching behind me several years before. I would do my best in the classroom but I was there more as a traveller than as a teacher. It would be me who'd be doing most of the learning, in and outside of school.

And so I was lacking the zeal of my British neighbour whom I spoke to before I entered my first class at Chindunduma. She had exclaimed, as we walked along the stone path in the blistering heat, "It's so exciting. We have so much to offer these poor kids." All this confidence, I thought, as she told me this was her first teaching assignment. I answered, "Oh, a few," when she had asked if I had many years' teaching experience.

I had learned that you cannot teach anybody anything, except by chance, until you get to know their needs. At that stage I didn't know how old my students were, how much English they understood, what they had learned at school in previous years or what their interests were. Those, then, were my objectives on that first day. And I was ready to have that phase last several weeks if necessary.

My timetable indicated that one of my courses was 'Lower Sixth, English, General Paper.' What did this mean? I wondered. The students told me just before the class began that it meant two classes per week, with about seventy pupils in their first year of the difficult Cambridge A levels. I was to teach them writing and speaking skills. Each class was thirty-five minutes in length. Somebody had to be joking!

These senior students had chosen not to take English as one of their three A Level subjects. The idea of this course seemed to be that they would at least improve the basics—reading, writing and speaking—all in about one hour per week. I calculated that I could probably accomplish little more than learning their names in the first semester.

What made those classes palatable—even fun—was that the students knew that the course was a farce. Over the years, those two classes every week had become a debating society, a forum. Students were eager to ask me questions about Canada and about myself. I decided to go with the flow. I'd learn about them in the process.

The first question came from a tall, strapping fellow sitting on top of a desk at the back of the room: "What type of aphrodisiacs are commonly used in Canada?" Well, when I finished my double-take, I managed to reply, "Oh, probably the same as here." This fence-sitting answer brought the house down. What had I said? The students howled.

They knew I was hedging. So I tried again, mentioning using alcohol, or perhaps marijuana, trying to get them talking. I was taken aback, especially when I noted the seriousness with which they were taking the discussion. There was no snickering. This was serious stuff: How did Canadians get themselves in the mood to enjoy sex?

Other questions followed, not always on the subject of sex. Money and politics were prominent. As were questions about freedoms and laws. These students —ranging in age from eighteen to twenty-eight—were curious. They wanted to know about clothes, food and medical treatment. Some wanted a map drawn to show where in 'Europe' Canada was located. Some wanted to know when and how Canadians obtained their independence. A difficult question to answer for a group of African kids used to hearing about coups and revolutions.

How much does a television cost? How much are school fees? What are uniforms like in schools? What do teachers use to beat students who misbehave? Could they see photographs of my children? How much does the average Canadian earn? Is there prostitution? Does everybody do military service? How many wives can a man take? To what extent did Canada suffer from 'the evils of capitalism?'

Intriguing questions. The half-hour went by in a flash. I had asked a student to act as recorder and I noted that there were enough topics on her list to last a whole term.

In subsequent classes, I was to receive my own education about life in their country. Only one student in the class could boast of having a television at home. Only one-third of the students had even visited Harare, about three hours away. Many of the male students had done military service during the war of independence (they would have been fourteen or fifteen years old at the time!).

Many were orphans, thanks again to that ten-year struggle. Some had scars which told of wounds and suffering. All believed in the efficacy of Marxist socialism, the cornerstone on which the new nation, now nine years old, had been built.

Above all, these young men and women were eager to learn. And they were unfailingly polite to me, as a teacher, and as a visitor to their country. I wondered how a class of Canadian students might receive a visiting Zimbabwean teacher. Here, they valued the chance to get an education, never mind of what quality. They actually liked having homework!

I started to care about them. I also started to care about the students in the thirty other periods I taught each week. I had told myself I wasn't going to let this happen; I wasn't going to take this seriously. I don't think I was being overly cynical. I realized I simply could not teach with any effectiveness in such a system. There were too many bodies in the classroom (often over fifty per class), too few books (usually one for every three students), too little paper, often no chalk and too much heat. Most discouraging of all was the students' glaring lack of background. The system was a travesty; students were routinely pushed ahead to each higher form and taught mainly by teachers who had never passed secondary school themselves. Brains were not the problem; these kids were intelligent. The absurdities of the education system often made me depressed and disillusioned—as the students continued to see me as a saviour.

But, at Chindunduma, I never stayed depressed for long. There was so much stimulation outside the classroom that it was easy to leave the job at school. There was the constant socializing on each other's front porches, informal dart tournaments, trips to the bottle store, to town. Perhaps it was the sheer hopelessness of the teaching situation which made everybody—except, sadly, the students—put it in the proper perspective. Most of us did what we could in class, then went home and forgot about it.

Except when Ngitimana called a staff meeting. He had the habit of summoning teachers for meetings around five in the afternoon. He, of course, knew that he was interfering with the 'cocktail hour' at Chindunduma. But he had a cruel streak in him.

Teachers would be alerted of the meeting by a messenger who would bang on your front door until you emerged, hand you a notice to read, then insist that you sign beside your name, making it pretty difficult to say the next day, "Sorry I missed the meeting, headmaster. I did not know about it."

The five o'clock meeting invariably began about six. Everybody was disgruntled, most had downed a beer or two before coming and everyone had somewhere else he or she preferred to be.

The morale, therefore, at meetings was decidedly apathetic, if not hostile.

Ngitimana would solicit our attention. "Comrades, comrades, please come to order. There is much work to be done."

Before he got into gear, one of the senior teachers, usually a fellow, ex-guerilla fighter, would say something like, "With your permission, comrade headmaster, I suggest that some serious consideration be given the matter of the upcoming Christmas party before moving on to the agenda."

Amid the ripple of laughter, Ngitimana would say, "Comrade Munatsi, not everyone here shares your interest in frivolity." More laughter. "We are here for one reason, and one reason only, that being to educate our charges. And comrades, it may be easy for you to take this lightly, but if our examination results are not vastly improved this term, I can tell you that heads will roll!"

That would bring on waves of laughter. More than half the thirty teachers present would light up cigarettes and settle in for a good time.

Munatsi, though, would not give in so easily. Something about the last year's Christmas party had upset him. Apparently, the beer had run out early, much to his chagrin. Munatsi was a drinker of prodigious proportions, perhaps a twenty-bottle-a-night man, as legend had it.

Indeed, he had consumed a few before the meeting. He was intent upon looking after his vested interest. That he was Dean of Students was beside the point, that exams were just around the corner, irrelevant. Not only that, he had the undivided attention of the whole staff. Who could contemplate another partially dry party? It was unthinkable.

Ngitimana knew he was beaten. He sighed, looked at his watch and agreed to discuss beer for "five minutes, comrades, and not a second more."

A half hour later, things were heating up. It seemed that last year at the party, certain staff members had been seen passing the precious, ice-cold bottles of Castle out the window to their support staff friends who were not included in the Christmas party, having had their own, all-night affair earlier.

"I suggest that the windows be secured in a closed position for the evening," offered one mischievous teacher, guffawing.

Another appealed for the admission of the support staff to this year's party, adding, "They will have to include us in theirs, too, comrades." He was dreaming of a double beer-drink. Naturally, everybody agreed. That way, we could help decimate their beer supply, and they could do the same for us.

Important matters, indeed. An hour went by. My eyes began to burn from the cigarette smoke permeating the room.

Finally, the headmaster got to introduce his first item of business. It concerned the upcoming Parents' Day. It was the big event of the school year. Imagine, bussing in the parents of over seven hundred students, none of whom owned a car. Most would come from rural areas across the region. They would come not so much to inquire about the progress of their progeny, rather they would come because they knew the school always provided a hearty meal for them.

"Last year, I received complaints about the size of meat portions, comrades. This was embarrassing," Ngitimana said, "and it must not happen again. My head will roll should there be a repeat of last year's sad experience."

I wondered if the parents consumed meat as their children's teachers consumed beer. If so, I doubted there was enough beef in Zimbabwe to fill the requirement. And I wondered when an 'education' item might be brought up at the meeting as I noticed the hoards of students heading for the study halls after supper, their teachers intent only on the business of food and drink.

A decision was made to take the school lorry to Harare the day before Parents' Day for the sole purpose of fetching a load of beef, duly carved and packaged for the edification of hungry parents. Several teachers selflessly offered to go along for the ride. The truck would be sure to stop at every bottle store along the way. No matter that the loaded beef would fry on the back of the lorry in the blistering afternoon sun.

"And now, comrades, as most of you are, no doubt, hungry yourselves, we shall rush right along."

Several teachers lit up again. I edged towards an open window, gasping for air. This was going to be a marathon. I guessed we would now tackle some pressing education problems.

The headmaster continued. "Comrade Munyati, we are all interested in the health of your wife."

The health of Munyati's wife? What about the lack of books for third form English? Or the shortage of chalk?

"She is much improved, thank you, headmaster," Munyati answered, with a wry smile. He suspected something was up. He knew the headmaster intimately, having served in the army of liberation with him in the hills for ten years or so. Munyati knew he was being set up. "We all know that malaria is usually nothing to worry about. In this case, I am happy to report that my wife is well on the road to recovery."

This was greeted by a round of pleased utterances from the gathered teachers. But they too knew that the headmaster had something else in mind. We all soon found out.

"We are all relieved to hear this, comrade," said Ngitimana. "No doubt you will not be quite so occupied with looking after your household now that your wife is getting better." A ripple of knowing laughter went through the assembled crowd.

"That is true," answered Munyati, "and not a minute too soon. As you know many of my classes are preparing for final examinations. I am worried about them. They are weak, so weak. I will have to give them every spare moment of my attention in the weeks ahead." Everyone nodded in sympathy. That the students were weak was not debatable.

"Of course, comrade, and so must we all," the headmaster responded, pursing his lips in a demeanour of extreme seriousness. "And yet, there is the immediate question which I know is uppermost in all your minds."

We looked at each other blankly. Had something happened with the payroll system? Hell, what could happen to it? It wasn't working anyway. Pay cheques always arrived late, or not at all.

"I am referring, of course, to the matter of designating someone to act as Master of Ceremonies for this year's Parents' Day."

Some audible groans. Not more Parents' Day nonsense! The pacifying effects of the pre-meeting drinks were starting to dissipate.

"We all know how demanding parents are," Ngitimana reminded us, shaking his head, remorsefully.

My British colleague, Nick, leaned over and whispered, "Sure as hell are, mate. They demand double portions of nyama or they'll raise bloody hell." Everybody had developed the habit of using a smattering of Shona words in everyday speech.

"They expect to be not only informed of the workings of the school in educating their offspring, but demand to be—how shall I say—entertained as well. And we all know what a fine job Comrade Munyati did as M.C. last year," Ngitimana bellowed, trying to be heard above the rising din.

So this was it. Ngitimana was trying to con Munyati into doing the onerous job of acting as M.C. again this year. I had heard that he was routinely given the job because he could always be counted on to loosen the crowd up. Rural people tend to be a bit reticent, subdued. Munyati apparently changed all that. He had told jokes in Shona which had them rolling in the isles. The fact that he had been quite inebriated was irrelevant. He was going to be this year's M.C. too, like it or not.

He did not like it.

"Sir, I thank you for the kind words," Munyati responded. "Rest assured that no one knows the importance of our Parents' Day more than I. As you once said, comrade, we all must not only do a good job here at Chindunduma, but we must be seen to do a good job."

This brought a round of snickers from the group. Munyati was putting Ngitimana on, but he wasn't over-doing it.

"Exactly, comrade, exactly," the headmaster smiled broadly, adding, "and you did us all proud when you volunteered to act as M.C. last year."

More giggles. Munyati had been fingered to do the job last year, too, and was so angry that he had gotten loaded early in the morning, hoping he'd screw up so badly he'd never be asked again. Ironically, he'd been the hit of the day!

"I believe the headmaster is aware of the reason for last year's successful Open House," Munyati said, before pausing to add, "it was the excellent meal of sadza and nyama. That is all those people judge us by."

Howls of laughter. Nods of agreement.

"Comrades, conduct yourselves with professionalism. Let us be serious," Ngitimana scolded. "We all recall the refined oratorical skills of comrade Munyati and his, well, his special rapport with the parents."

It became clear Ngitimana was not going to back down. Munyati, for his part, was probably getting thirsty for another beer. Indeed, everybody wanted out of the meeting. It was now after eight o'clock. This was definitely cutting into the social hour.

It might seem as though too big a fuss was being made over a simple job of being M.C. The big fuss was warranted; an African Parents' Day began about eight in the morning and lasted until almost dusk. There were constant activities —student performances, demonstrations, interviews—but mostly the parents expected to be entertained when they weren't being fed. It was a case of being somewhat 'reimbursed' for paying their children's school fees. Munyati, even drunk, was just the medicine needed. Maybe especially drunk.

Munyati may have even wanted the job. We were all witnessing a ritual being carried out. It had taken time, but it had been entertaining.

Not surprising, it was the only item on the agenda! The meeting adjourned. The real problems—student needs—could wait until next time.

And, oh yes, one other item was discussed before adjournment. After accepting the M.C. job, Munyati had sneaked a request by the headmaster which had delighted everyone present. He had extracted a promise of transportation by school lorry for teachers to the bottle store right after the parents left for home. Sort of a treat for all of us after the stresses involved in meeting the parents. Munyati was a hero already.

We filed out of the meeting, a cool evening breeze instantly assuaging the stinging eyes of the non-smokers. Staff meetings, parties, transportation problems, my classes—all added up to a priceless savouring of Zimbabwean culture. Amid the failings of the education system—which you don't have to go to Africa to experience—I came to know, living and working at Chindunduma, a people who were warm, sensitive and, most of all, fun-loving.

The Pungwe—What a Riot!

There was a sameness about life at Chindunduma that necessitated periodic trips to the city as an antidote to 'cabin fever.' On one of these escapes to Harare we attended a Pungwe.

A Pungwe (pronounced, poongway) is a concert which usually features the best musicians in Zimbabwe and is really a gigantic party which goes on until the sun comes up or everybody drops, whichever comes first.

The Pungwe had its origins in the war of liberation when freedom fighters would come out of the hills and visit villages in order to inform the people about the happenings in their struggle with the Rhodesian government. Guerilla fighters would talk, but they'd also lead the villagers in songs—songs of freedom or of inspiration designed to fire the people up.

We were excited about attending the show at Rufaro Stadium, in the heart of a so-called high-density area which had been a desperately poor slum before liberation. Now it was still a ghetto, overcrowded, all black and—if I believed a couple of guys who whispered, "What you doing here, brother?", as we made our way through the turnstiles at the stadium—perhaps dangerous for outsiders.

The headliner for tonight's show was none other than Thomas Mapfumo, the biggest name in Zimbabwean music, a sort of Bob Dylan of southern Africa. We had company—Nick, along with his passion for music, and his Zimbabwean girlfriend, Rosaline.

The four of us arrived about ten o'clock. We didn't want to peak too soon. There was a mob of people outside the stadium and, in true African fashion, there was only one gate open. People were admitted one at a time as they were herded through a wire mesh. Three kids tried to pick my pocket as we slowly made our way along. Other youths were climbing the wire fence, in monkey fashion, as police whacked furiously at them with truncheons.

It was eerie—seeing nothing but the concrete bowl of the huge stadium as we entered, it was as if no one was there—but as we made our way down to the infield, we could see several thousands, many dancing wildly to the Mapfumo beat. The stage was set up at one end of the soccer field. Thomas and his band of about six musicians, called Blacks Unlimited, accompanied by four women dancers, were in high gear.

We let Nick and Ros lead the way as Ros had been here before. I had as yet seen no other whites inside the stadium. As we meandered our way through the crowd, I could feel the people's stares. I felt uneasy.

The two women and I sat on the infield and waited for Nick to return with drinks. Several hulking guys hovered around us, continuing to stare us down. When Nick returned, it became obvious why the kids hung around: they wanted us to share our beer. We declined on Ros' advice. "They see you people, and automatically expect a hand-out."

I knew who she meant by "you people."

Thomas Mapfumo is a fine musician, very thin, charismatic and talented. He is an old pro, prominent back in the days of the liberation struggle when the authorities officially banned his songs. It was then that he went underground and surfaced at pungwes all over the country.

This Pungwe was going to be different from an American or Canadian rock concert. Thomas spoke hardly a word. He and his band just played. The people obviously loved him, but did not outwardly show it. No round of applause followed the conclusion of his songs. People simply paused in their dancing to drink and catch their breath.

The crowd was anything but laid back though. A sense of joy and excitement pervaded. Like the music, everything was full throttle and non-stop. Finally, after about two hours of uninterrupted playing, the band took a break. For about ten minutes.

During that time, several small skirmishes broke out. I suspect they were all alcohol-related, mostly family squabbles, perhaps quarrels over women. I could see this could get ugly as the evening wore on. I spotted about three other whites in the large crowd. Our eyes met, but we said nothing.

Cops patrolled the infield; certainly more gun-toters than you'd see at a Bruce Springsteen concert. There were over ten thousand people present, I guessed.

It was a bizarre scene: a mob of people milling about a soccer field ringed by a mini-army! We might have been political prisoners awaiting execution, or transportation to a detention camp.

We decided to move to another part of the stadium, hoping to land among more sedate types. Now it was my turn to join the beer line-up.

The music started up again. Somehow, I felt more secure now. The beat of Mapfumo induces a feeling of warmth and security. It exudes spirituality. After a half-hour, I was nearing the beer coolers.

It was then I heard what I thought were firecrackers exploding. From my vantage point in the stands, I could see little puffs of smoke rising from the infield. I hadn't noticed that the music had stopped a few minutes before, and some words had been spoken over the loudspeaker.

I got my supply of beer and headed down to the infield. I did not advance very far. More explosions. More smoke. I asked a sober fellow nearby what was happening.

"It's the fucking cops," he said. "They've started shooting and using tear gas!"

"Why?" I gasped.

"Seems the authorities went and cancelled the show," he went on. "Something about the organizers failing to obtain the right licence. Christ! My wife is down there."

My heart sank. So was mine. I could only see larger clouds of smoke. Now there was screaming and yelling. My companion yelled, "Hit the dirt, brother!"

I concurred, as I realized bullets were zinging close by. I don't think I have ever been so frightened. Were Elaine, Nick and Ros all caught in the middle? Had they been trampled? The chaos was incredible. Shooting. Screaming. Pushing. I covered my head with my arms, following the lead of my guide.

I could see a phalanx of police ringing the infield. I could also see why they had started shooting. Disappointed fans, all very drunk, had trashed the stage after the announcement of the cancellation, and had then begun throwing pieces of equipment at the police, whom they perceived as the bad guys, the enforcers of the decision to call off the Pungwe.

Bottles had become the weapon of choice. It was scary. I could see blood-covered faces a short distance away. Should I stay and be trampled? Try to find the others? Run towards the exit? I recalled the single-file entrance, and shuddered. Surely someone would open some of the exit gates.

So far, there seemed to be only hysteria. Women's screams pierced my ears. This was a nightmare.

I must have stayed on the ground for twenty minutes. The shooting was now sporadic and things seemed to be calming down somewhat, although there was still an atmosphere of mayhem. People around me seemed to be heading for an exit nearby. I decided against finding my mates, opting instead to try to get out of the stadium. I could only pray that Nick, Ros and Elaine would also make it to safety. If they were still mobile . . .

In a matter of minutes, I was outside the stadium. Police sirens wailed. Ambulances were rushing to the scene. It was ironic to feel safe right in the middle of Mbare. But compared to inside the stadium, this was tranquil. I headed in the direction of the city centre, about six kilometres away. The streets were crowded. Probably most were feeling as I was: worried about loved ones.

I made it in an hour to a bus stop where I hopped a bus for the remainder of the trip into town.

A steady stream of ambulances and police vehicles clogged the road heading in the other direction.

I decided to go directly to the little hotel where we were staying for the night. As I feared, the others had not made it back. Still, considering their location in the stadium when the riot broke out, that was not surprising.

I paced back and forth on the verandah. The proprietor was incredulous as I shared my story of the evening with him. He kept shaking his head.

"Our people have never learned how to cope with power," he said.

"How do you mean?"

"Well, what kind of idiots order a Pungwe in full swing to be shut down because somebody forgot to fill out a form?" he asked lividly. "You see, my friend, we never had to do anything but be slaves for the oppressors. Now we are like children pretending to be adults. It is all very sad."

I couldn't concentrate on the man's analysis of the country's problems. I just wanted to see Elaine, Nick and Ros walk up the path.

Two hours went by. I jumped every time the phone rang, praying it would be for me.

It must have been four o'clock in the morning when a taxi pulled up. I held my breath.

I was elated to see Elaine climb out, followed by Nick. Finally Ros emerged, looking as though she had been through a war. Her arm was in a sling, her face heavily bandaged.

But she was smiling. So were they all as they spotted me.

Elaine threw her arms around me, sobbing, "I'm so glad you're safe. We were frantic about you. I tried to call, but there were line-ups at every phone booth."

"Where were you?" I asked.

"At the hospital. Ros was hurt. It wasn't as bad as it first appeared; she has only a broken arm and a gash on her forehead from a flying beer bottle."

"She's very fortunate, mate," Nick added. "We saw one guy shot dead within ten feet of where we were sitting. And at the hospital—well, it looked like a bloody war zone!"

Everybody was wound up, all talking at once. It turned out that the riot had left six people dead and dozens injured. We were lucky, indeed.

Our Pungwe riot provided the stuff of many late-night conversations on the porch at Chindunduma. And perhaps we realized, during those periods of sameness and boredom, that there were worse things to cope with than 'cabin fever.'

Back in the Promised Land

After returning to Canada from Zimbabwe, I had some difficulty adjusting to 'life at home.' My feelings are probably best expressed in the following piece I wrote for the *Globe and Mail*. I include it here because, at the time, selling even a single article was a boost to an ego deflated after finding all employment doors closed. My job at Creative Services was then six months down the road.

A SOCIETY OF SIDETRACKED VALUES
By Jim Shannon

I spent some time in Africa recently. I was teaching and living at a rural school in Zimbabwe, and the experience was one of the most stimulating of my life. Learning to live without a car, telephones, television sets, movies and shopping malls was an opportunity to savour a new culture.

To say that I came to prefer the lifestyle of an expatriate teacher in the African bush would be simplistic. After all, being without power for twenty-four hours after you've just done your weekly grocery shopping trip, by the slowest bus imaginable, to the nearest town about sixty kilometres away, is no joke.

There was the isolation. And lack of privacy. The heat and the overcrowded and under-equipped classrooms. And the three-week wait for letters from home. The dearth of reading material. And the underlying racial tension.

Yet, I found life there to be more real, more "hands on," simpler than the life I had left behind in Canada.

Like most of my foreign colleagues—there were eight white teachers on the staff, along with twenty-five Zimbabweans—I came to appreciate the warmth of the local people. I learned to talk to passers-by who were genuinely interested in my life. I learned to make do with a meal of pasta and assorted vegetables gathered by stopping at neighbours' gardens on a late-afternoon walk the day before a trip to town to buy supplies. A barter system operated: "Thanks for the carrots and tomatoes. I'll bring you back some beer on my next trip to town."

Evenings became social events. People would drop in, unannounced, and a party would ensue. We'd often talk well into the night. I got to know those Zimbabweans better than I know my neighbours and co-workers at home. In those long evenings on our porch, people became amazingly candid. One would tell of sending most of his pay cheque to his parents to help support the family even though he had a wife and kids at Chindunduma. He, in turn, would quiz me about my life in Ottawa, gasping with incredulity when I explained that Canada gives financial assistance to its jobless, its poor, its infirm and its aged. And that every household boasts at least one television set.

A hitchhiking venture into town would invariably reap a social benefit—an invitation to someone's home for dinner or an offer to have a tour of a game park. Time was nothing in Africa, much to the disdain of many foreigners who failed to change gears.

I cannot say I adapted right away. But I'm glad I handled the culture shock I first felt when I got off the plane in Harare one stiflingly hot night, hungry, tired and frustrated after a flight that was ten hours late. The long, bumpy ride in the back of a truck to the school in the bush didn't help either. Welcome to Africa!

I had trouble adjusting to not having my own car. Transportation was a real problem. A missed ride could mean spending the night sleeping on the floor of the nearest bottle store, thirty kilometres away. But the owner was friendly and the beer was cold. And the mosquitoes never gave me malaria though they bit all night long.

If life in Zimbabwe was so difficult, then why did I have such a hard time adjusting to life back in Canada?

Several things struck me upon re-entry. Necessities of life were outrageously expensive. People seemed cold and distant, hardly ever speaking or making eye contact on the street. Everybody was in a hurry. People talked of nothing but their possessions. There was discord. My fellow countrymen, French and English, whites and native peoples, were at each other's throats. There were too many cars, shopping malls, credit cards, television channels, noise, crime. Even taxes. There was too much of everything. Or too much of nothing, as a line in a Bob Dylan song suggested.

The life I had experienced in Africa seemed to magnify the excesses, the preoccupation with consuming and the coldness and lack of colour in Canadian life. Faces of people on the street reflected a malaise missing in the people I had been meeting during the previous year.

Didn't everybody and his uncle in the Third World long to come to America, which is what my African friends persisted in calling Canada?

I recalled the reasons my Zimbabwean colleagues gave for dreaming of leaving their land of the perfect climate for the Cold White North. They invariably spoke of their desire for safety, for order and justice. In African states, even the more advanced ones like Zimbabwe and Kenya, any criticism of the government brings down some sort of retaliation—a lost job, a knock on the door in the middle of the night, a mysterious disappearance or being tossed in jail.

Here I can openly criticize my government, even poke fun at the prime minister. My friends at the school pointed out that even failing to refer to their president by his full name of Robert Gabriel Mugabe—or forgetting to pull off the road should his entourage be passing—would result in repercussions.

I can use my union at work to redress wrongs. Press charges against anyone harming me or my family and depend on police protection without having to pay them a bribe. Walk the streets of even the largest Canadian cities with little fear of being robbed or mugged. Yes, I live in a free, orderly society.

The other reason Third World people give for wanting to emigrate to Canada is the abundance of opportunities. For some, that meant a better chance to practise a profession but, upon further discussion, it came to mean the chance to make more money. To buy material goods. These people had the necessities. They were speaking of the 'extras.' You need money to buy VCRs, compact disc players, second cars, big houses, designer clothing and so on.

How have Africans been seduced by Western-style consumerism? Perhaps by television, even though few families there have one; by seeing how the 'haves' in their own countries (i.e., the whites) live; by seeing what tourists value. The line-up forms at immigration.

And so, I wondered, if so many of my fellow Canadians and virtually all my Third World friends saw Canada in such glowing light, what was wrong with me? Why was I seeing things so negatively? I enjoy the 'good life' as much as anyone. It was the excessiveness that struck me.

After a while, will the newcomers to Canada perceive the excesses and long to be back home where life is simpler? Will they be turned off by the obsession of Canadians with consumer goods?

Life is easy here; we are free, society is orderly. We can get bitten by a mosquito without worrying about contracting malaria. Go for a walk at night without worrying about stepping on a sleeping cobra, as I once did. We can take public transportation and be confident a tire won't blow out. We can even lose our jobs and be temporarily taken care of. Get sick and receive free treatment. Indeed, we have everything.

One other thing we have now is greater cultural diversity, thanks to the influx of these immigrants. If we're open, we could learn something from the newcomers from lands where life is simpler. We could learn to slow down a bit, relax and enjoy our lives. Savour the simple things.

Perhaps we do live in the Promised Land. We've just gotten a little sidetracked.

Back at the office where, readers will recall, I was busy marking time at Creative Services, my 'designated resignation day' was fast approaching. The recollection of those African adventures shored up my determination to once again take The Plunge, leave a job I knew was not right for me. I remembered how I felt riding the elevator to the Olympic Stadium press box to start my job as a baseball writer. I recalled my first glimpse of India; the old woman leading us through the streets of Belgrade to our bed in her kitchen; hopping the Orient Express in Paris; riding in the back of the school truck to Chindunduma; driving Sonny to the hospital in Negril.

There was, indeed, a world beyond the Ottawa office tower. Time was too precious to waste.

In mid-November, with a freezing rain pelting the windows, I walked into Sylvia's office and—shades of a day almost ten years before—said, "Sylvia, I'm outta here!"

Ten Years After

When I recall taking The Plunge ten years ago, I realize that I had no clear idea what I was getting into, but that I was somehow willing to take the risks involved.

Changing aspects of life—be they jobs, relationships, habits—which are unsuitable, even destructive, is often difficult and frightening. No wonder so many of us opt to accept so much less than we can have! We deserve more. We owe it to ourselves to find contentment.

Robert Anton Wilson said, "The only reason most people remain in the same jobs, the same towns, the same belief-systems year after year is, of course, that cultural conditioning, in every tribe, is a process of gradually narrowing your tunnel-reality." He advocates "taking a quantum leap every so often and landing yourself in a new reality-matrix" as the way of avoiding this pitfall.

Those words are idealistic, I admit. Giving up the familiar—even when it is unsatisfying—is no easy task. Yet, the rewards are great. The travels I undertook, the people I met and the work experiences I had over the last ten years have enriched my life immeasurably. Had I not taken the chance, gambled that there was a new life for me after forty, then I'd be wallowing in the same quagmire of routine, boredom and fear that I now see many of my old friends and colleagues stuck in. I feel I 'did it' just in time! Changes are harder to make as we get older.

What surprises me now is not that I was able to leave behind the familiar and the secure (drop a stale career in my case) and leap into unknown territory, but that *everybody* who is dissatisfied with some major aspect of life doesn't do it. Carl Jung put it well: "We should not lead the second half of our lives using the same principles that we used in the first half." We need different tools, or maps, to survive and flourish at various stages in our lives. Unfortunately, many of us tend to let the 'robot' take over as we get on one treadmill or another and just hang on.

The key to liberating ourselves is learning not to judge ourselves by commonly accepted 'societal yardsticks.' It is not others we have to listen to; it is 'that voice inside of us' that must be heeded. Bob Marley put it well in one of his songs: "Emancipate yourselves from mental slavery,/ None but ourselves can free our minds." Achieving this mental freedom requires patience and, above all, determination.

I don't know what the future holds. It may be a new work experience or travel to some long-dreamt-of exotic destination. The inner voice may say, "Why not just wander? There's so much of the world you haven't seen." Then again, the next adventure may be staring me in the face, right here at home.

Finally, if you're discontented with the track you're on—having looked at it from all angles and still found it lacking—then get off it and forge a new one. I hope *Once Again, At Forty* has encouraged readers to get moving before it's too late.

Appendix

A Survival Reading List

I hope *ONCE AGAIN, AT FORTY* has inspired readers, as I mentioned earlier, to begin, or to continue, making those vital, necessary changes in their lives that will result in greater fulfillment. To do that, we need all the help we can get. Books are prominent on my own list of survival necessities. I'll try to convey the essence of a few of those I've found most helpful.

Somerset Maugham, in *The Razor's Edge,* provides an excellent model of a person striving to carve out his own path. His main character, Larry, is an evolved young man who has a thirst for knowledge. He is capable of following his instincts and opts for a life of intense study, travel and adventure.

M. Scott Peck, in *The Road Less Traveled,* gives perhaps the best survival tip of all: Stop being lazy. Peck calls the force of laziness within us entropy. Much fear is masked in laziness. Fears are often of a change in the status quo, a fear that we may lose what we have if we venture forth from where we are now. We have to "revise our outdated maps," and we usually seek to avoid this painful work. Realizing the power of our will, Peck insists, allows us to carry out the necessary changes.

The Indian philosopher, Krishnamurti, in *The Urgency of Change,* complements Peck as he cautions us to look at things closely. First observe, he says. Don't worry about planning or seeking solutions. The future will take care of itself if we can only learn to become "choicelessly aware." Man's downfall is his (or her) inability to see the world "always as if seeing it for the first time." We tend to lose our innate capacity of "responding freshly to everything" as we grow up. Krishnamurti urges us to get rid of this "automatic pilot."

Stephen Levine's book, *A Gradual Awakening,* looks at the problem of focusing the mind, of being aware. We must learn to experience things as they *are.* Meditation helps us balance the mind so that it can shine through and get away from conceptual thought forms projected by desire and conditioning. Being focused is of paramount importance. Levine's gimmicky-free method of meditation continues to be useful.

In *Modern Man in Search of his Soul,* Carl Jung stresses that we should devote more time to establishing a better relationship with our unconscious, that part of us that is normally neglected as we tackle the outside world, become educated, get established and so on. We can do this by paying more attention to our dreams which contain information, or messages, from that part of our mind, often long-neglected.

Colin Wilson, in two excellent books, *Access to Inner Worlds* and *Carl Jung: Lord of the Underworld*, proves a lucid interpreter of Jung's ideas, reinforcing the contention that the unconscious is an enormous wellspring of vital forces.

Joseph Campbell, in *An Open Life*, says that, for many of us, the sense of the vitality of life has gone. He advocates examining archetypal myths as a means of finding the dynamic force in our life. He says we must find the courage to follow the 'process.' In order to have something new, something old must be broken, and if you're too heavily fixed on the old, you're going to get stuck. We must somehow become childlike, full of spontaneity and hope.

In India, he says, a man lives the first half of his life in society, obeying the rules, following the dictates of his caste and worshipping the local images of divine power. But then he goes into the forest, gives up his caste, or position, and concerns himself with the spiritual aspect of his life.

As a traveller, a book I alluded to in an earlier chapter, Brian Schwartz's, *A World Of Villages*, continues to inspire me to travel as much as possible and to experience the wonders of our planet. He advocates travel "not to discover myself, but to meet my fellow man."

E.F. Schumacher, in *Small is Beautiful*, writes of the importance of putting our "inner house" in order. The guidance we need for this work, he said, can be found not in science and technology, but rather in the traditional wisdom of mankind. "Keep it simple," he advises. A simple life makes demands upon us which, in the long run, serve to keep us vigilant, active, alive.

Aldous Huxley, in both *Brave New World* and *Time Must Have a Stop*, points out that self-knowledge is an essential prerequisite to self-change. If reflexes can be conditioned, they can be reconditioned. Learning to use the self properly when one has been using it badly, depends on our reconditioning our reflexes.

We must learn to live in the present, never in the past or the future; life here, now, not life looked forward to or recollected.

A recent book, *The Joy of Not Working*, by Ernie J. Zelinski, deserves mention. It's not as frivolous as the title may imply. If you are too hung up on the Protestant Work Ethic, this book is a good antidote. I wish I'd had access to such a book over a decade ago when I was contemplating quitting my job and trying to muster up the courage to do so.

Finally, Hugh MacLennan, in his novel, *The Watch That Ends the Night*, reminds us of the mysteries of life:

"There is no simple explanation for anything important any of us do, and the human tragedy, or human irony, consists in the necessity of living with the consequences of actions performed under the pressure of compulsions so obscure we do not and cannot understand them . . . God gave life. He gave it. Life for a year, a month, a day or an hour is still a gift. The warmth of the sun or the caress of the air, the sight of a flower or a cloud on the wind, the possibility of even for one more day to see things grow—the human bondage is also the human liberty . . . To have that understanding, to feel the movement of light flood the darkness, even for an instant, is the most beautiful experience in the world . . . To be able to love the mystery surrounding us is the final and only sanction of human existence."

These are a few of the books which have helped me forge my own path—my Survival Reading List.

Appendix

Financial Matters

"But how do you guys live?" So asked a fellow traveller during a chat on a beach in Jamaica. He didn't believe me when I gave him a thumb-nail sketch of our lives over the last ten years. How could Elaine and I have survived, working only periodically and doing all that travelling?

Yes, money is important in everybody's life. Nevertheless, I have resisted the temptation to write a "How-to-Arrange-your-Finances" chapter. Everyone's circumstances are different—number and ages of children, annual income, material requirements, debts, roles of spouses/partners, etc. "How much is enough?" remains a primary question in everyone's life.

I went on to tell my beach acquaintance who, like many people, was fed up with a dreary, stale career, that I had perceived changing my life as my main task at hand when I decided to Take the Plunge. If there is a 'why,' then you can find the 'how.' Some sacrifices may be necessary.

I could only assure him that the things he is probably now worrying about will recede far into the background as he proceeds along a new path. I tried to illustrate my point by briefly outlining my own experience.

For a few years before I left my job, I made a concerted effort to clear my debts, to save some money, to bring down my living costs. I was, at that time, a separated parent and was fortunate to have an ex-wife who was sharing in the financial requirements of the children. I lived in cheaper housing (though never in a hovel), drove an older car, spent little on clothes and electronic goodies.

My only extravagence was travel, and I became a budget traveller early on. I discovered I could live on a fraction of my teacher pay cheque. Hence, when I quit my job, I managed to support myself and my children adequately without ever having a 9 to 5 job for any appreciable length of time.

Housing presented problems. If you're travelling—or working abroad—for a part of each year, do you maintain a house or apartment while you're on the road? Not usually. We sublet our apartment sometimes. We put our furniture and personal effects in storage (often in friends' basements). We suffered the inconvenience of having to find new lodgings after travels of a longer duration than a few months.

But the benefits of being 'unsettled' are many: we have lived in eight or nine different houses/apartments/cottages over the last decade; our lives have been enriched by the experience of frequent moving—new neighbourhoods, neighbours, friends.

Finding enough work to keep a cash flow was not always easy. But again, we persevered. Elaine went back to nursing periodically; I, to substitute teaching. We both did jobs we'd never dreamed of doing: I worked in carpentry and landscaping; she, as a letter carrier and in personnel. Change is the essence of life, as I said before! And it gets easier if you don't become too 'stuck.'

Finally, I explained to my questioner that, without being a player of the stock market, I managed to live for periods of time off the income from a few well-placed investments, using the tax benefits of cashing RRSPs in years of lower income, and so on. As I mentioned in Chapter One, my 'nest egg' was not large. It consisted of about six months' salary ("vested sick leave") which I received from my employer upon 'retirement' and promptly put into an RRSP; and about the same amount in pension contributions which I withdrew and also rolled over into an RRSP; and under $10,000 in savings. I have never owned a house. I have never had a rich uncle leave me a fortune. Ten years later, even with my frequent nibbling at these investments, they are now worth significantly more than they totalled at the start!

And so, suffice to say, you usually have to give up something to get something in return, but money is the last reason you should have for not taking the steps necessary to change your life.

About the Author

Jim Shannon was born in Marmora, Ontario in 1941. He lives in Ottawa where he works as a freelance writer. His work has appeared in the Globe and Mail, the Toronto Star and the Ottawa Citizen. He is currently working on his next book and contemplating his next trip.